Dear White Christian:

What Every White Christian Needs to Know about How Black Christians See, Think, & Experience Racism in America

Respectfully written by a black Christian

Aaron J. Layton

© 2017 - Committee on Discipleship Ministries
1700 North Brown Road, Suite 102
Lawrenceville, Georgia 30043
Bookstore: 1-800-283-1357
678-825-1100
www.pcacdm.org/bookstore

Database(C) 2001 iExalt, Inc.

ISBN: 978-1-944964-12-2

To my wife, Gretchen

To my son, Caleb

To my daughter, Kalei

and

To my parents,
Leroy and Geneva Layton

"That there may be no division in the body, but that the members may have the same care for one another. If one member suffers, all suffer together . . ."

1 Cor. 12:25-26

"I am thankful for this honest and open-hearted book from Aaron Layton, who has given his life to demonstrating that Christ's heart is large enough and strong enough to endure the hard conversations believers need to have in order to unite their hearts in him. Layton opens the conversation by opening his life to the examination of those would could not have shared his experiences in order to have all share the priorities of the gospel in the communities, families, and schools in which our God calls us to carry his Son's light."

Bryan Chapell
Pastor, Grace Presbyterian Church, Peoria, IL
President emeritus, Covenant Theological Seminary,
St. Louis, MO

"Issues regarding race and ethnicity, especially relating to the African-American community, continue to plague our nation with conflict and divisiveness that often seem to be irresolvable. So often misconceptions and lack of knowledge become barriers to peace, understanding, and hope. It is in this space that Christians and Christian communities are called to be the intentional peacemakers that will bring the Gospel to bear on the conflict and create real opportunities for reconciliation. The Christian community can and should be a model in bringing racial restoration and reconciliation to a broken world. In his book, "Dear White Christian," Aaron Layton provides a black leader's perspective on racial reconciliation; his teaching, experience, and insights help to break down the walls that inhibit real conversations and understanding to take place and help bring about positive change. "

James Marsh
Director, Van Lunen Center at Calvin College, Grand Rapids, MI
Head of school emeritus, Westminster Christian Academy, St. Louis, MO

"I commend "Dear White Christian" to all my brothers and sisters in Christ. Aaron asks us to, "please have the courage to lean into the discomfort of this book and allow it to challenge you in every way that God intends." You will be blessed if you take on this challenge. Aaron gives many tangible and helpful suggestions in putting the ideas of this book into practice in our local churches. You'll see this book doesn't just contain mere theoretical recommendations divorced from real life, but actual examples of how the principles and practices are being lived out. I appreciate most that this book is written by a brother who writes out of love for his readers, and who leads the way with his own willingness to face, admit, and grow from his own racial biases while also being vulnerable about pains he's suffered in his journey. Aaron is daily living out his challenge to "recognize the season we are in and steward it well." His book will help us all do the same."

Thurman L. Williams
Associate Pastor, Grace and Peace Fellowship
Church, St. Louis, MO
Adjunct faculty, Covenant Theological Seminary,
St. Louis, MO

Aaron Layton's "Dear White Christian" is a valuable contribution to our ongoing need for racial healing among God's people. Aaron's life experience in the cultures of the black inner city and white suburbia provides invaluable insights. He offers practical help that can facilitate transformational gospel conversations. Aaron provides honest feedback to white Christians to help expose the blind spots of limited experience and sinful prejudices in our hearts and in our white majority culture. His heart and counsel is an expression of James 1:19: "Know this, my beloved brothers and sisters, let every person be quick to hear, slow to speak, and slow to anger."

Mark Dalbey
President, Covenant Theological Seminary,
St. Louis, MO

Contents

Acknowledgements

There are just a few people I would like to thank although there are many more that I could thank. I would like to thank "The Queen," my wife Gretchen for the many years of support, love and faith in me. I would like to thank my children, Caleb and Kalei, for being patient with Dad for the many hours spent away from home helping others. I would also like to thank Andy Kerckhoff who thought I had something worth writing about, Luke Davis who helped me organize my thoughts, and Mike Weinberg who helped me understand the purpose for writing this book. Anne and Mark Derousse for allowing me to use their chalet at Innsbrook to write. Cindy Zavalgia for editing my manuscript, and Heather Marsee for formatting my manuscript. I would also like to thank Peggy Johnson, Jim Marsh, Scott Hickox, Michael Leary, Professor Greg Perry, Mike Higgins, Dave Schall, JD and Christan Perona, Lauren Simpson, Dan Burke, Sara DeVries, Karen Thompson, Scott Holley, Kelley Schwartz, Craig Walseth, Jason Thompson, Damion Jones, Pastor Tony Jeffrey, Sean Noble, Ed Thompson, Pastor Mike Jones, Greginald Summers, Pastor Carlos Mayfield, Courtney Peebles (JR), Pastor Barry Hennings, Pastor Tony Miles, Vince Bantu, Bryan Chapell, Professor Jerram Barrs, Professor David Chapman, Dr. Carl Ellis, and Professor Anthony Bradley.

Introduction

Never in my wildest dreams did I think I would be writing a book like this. Years ago, I told God I would never write a book unless he told me to, unless I thought I had something unique to share, and unless I thought it could really help someone or some group of people. All those things are true, so I am writing this book to help Christians—black and white—to move forward in the conversation of race relations and to reach out for a greater unity between one another.

To my white Christian brothers and sisters, I am writing primarily to you, but this is not a book that is designed to "beat you up" and make you feel guilty. This is a book written with the love of Christ. As one of my black college teammates, who is from the South, used to say to me, "You love you some white people, don't you?" Yes, it's true, I do. And despite experiencing the pain of racism at the hands of many whites in my life, Christ has allowed me to move past resentment and bitterness, although sometimes I am still challenged. I say all this in order that you would know that I am not an "angry black man," though I am a black man who does get angry at times. I consider myself to be even-tempered and reasonable, but also honest about the things I see as a black Christian.

It is my prayer that Christians, and white Christians in particular, will allow my book to inform them and challenge them about the way many black Christians view racism in America. The issues I express in this book are issues I believe most black Christians know, but they are also issues that every white Christian needs to know.

Many of the topics I mention are subjects that we as black Christians rarely share with our white Christian brothers and sisters for fear that we will be misunderstood, accused of exaggeration, told we are creating a problem by bringing up racial issues, or worse-ignored. So why would I dare write a book to white Christians? It is because we need a better way forward in the area of racial reconciliation.

For many years, we as black and white Christians have realized we need to get together and talk. I agree. However, I would add that we need to have the right type of conversation, and I am not convinced that the conversations of the past have helped us all that much. We need a conversation that is enlightening, compelling, and transformative. We need a conversation that is ongoing and helps us live out 1 Corinthians 12:25-26. ". . . that there may be no division in the body, but that the members may have the same care for one another. If one member suffers, all suffer together." Many black Christians, especially after the deaths of Trayvon Martin, Eric Garner, Tamir Rice, and Michael Brown, did not feel as though many of our white Christian brothers and sisters were suffering with us.

Our Racial Problem: Black and White Christians

It is no secret that the Christian church in America still suffers under the influence of racial bias. As a Christian, I would like to think that we are further along in the racism conversation in America. Yet I fear that as Christians we struggle in many of the same ways that many other white and black Americans do. In the current dialogues about racism, inequality, and police violence toward African Americans, our thoughts and conversations parallel those of non-believing white and black Americans.

After the death of Michael Brown and the riots in Ferguson that followed, many Americans were shocked and surprised. Americans wanted to believe that we as a country were further along in race relations than we actually were. To be fair, we have made strides as a nation, and yes, the fact that we had an African American President of the United States who served two terms indicates these strides. Nevertheless, the true test of race relations is what happens between races when there is a racial conflict.

Ferguson, Baltimore, and protests around the country reminded us that we still have much work to do as a nation. Not only did the Ferguson riots and the national protests surprise many white Americans, but it also surprised many white Christians.

After talking to a number of white Christians about the death of Michael Brown and the Ferguson riots, I learned that they too thought we were further along in race relations in America. As Christians, white and black, we have learned to coexist over the years without having the deeper, transformational, conversations of race with each other. I believe some of us have adopted the age old philosophy that believes talking about issues of race just makes things worse. However, this philosophy has not produced a greater unity among white and black Christians. We are just as polarized in our views of racism in America as non-believing whites and blacks, and the dialogue on social media after the death of Michael Brown illustrated it.

As Christians, as the body of Christ, we should and we can develop a deeper unity—a unity that is not so easily fractured when there is a Trayvon Martin or Michael Brown case. If we as Christians have the right conversations and begin to implement a long-term commitment to racial reconciliation in which we provide regular and intentional opportunities for our congregations and church leaders to grow in their understanding of racism in America, I think God will provide the Church in America an opportunity to get it right.

Please have the courage to lean into the discomfort of this book and allow it to challenge you in every way that God intends. I pray that this book will bring black and white Christians together to do the hard work of reconciliation and we would be able to stand together in the evil day. So let us begin the difficult, practical, and lengthy work of reconciliation—for true unity will cost us something.

1

The Divide

"The problem of the twentieth century is the problem of the color line."
—W. E. B. Du Bois[1]

I sat in my home church on a Sunday morning in August of 2014. I felt numb, still, and lifeless. It was a week after the death of Michael Brown and the Ferguson riots that followed.

The church was filled with white people. There were white people in front of me, white people behind me, and white people next to me. And although my church had always been filled with white people, that day somehow felt different. I felt different. I stared past my white pastor who was preaching his Sunday sermon. He was speaking, but I could no longer hear him. My mind had zeroed in on the fact that I was one of only four blacks present that morning.

Why did that matter all of a sudden? Why did it matter that there were not more blacks in our church that morning? My family and I had been attending the church for three years and were fully integrated into the community. I served as an elder, my wife helped serve communion, and both of my teenage children served in the children's church. But something had changed for me. Something had been revealed. Something had come to light. What was it?

[1] Du Bois, W.E.B., *The Souls of Black Folk* (Chicago: A.C. McClurg, 1903), V.

A Stark Reminder

Michael Brown was an eighteen year old, unarmed black male, who was fatally shot by Darren Wilson, a white, twenty-eight-year-old, Ferguson Police officer, on August 9, 2014 in Ferguson, Missouri. Brown's death generated a heated national debate about the relationship between law enforcement and African Americans, and about police use of force in Missouri and around the country. Michael Brown's death also sparked tensions in the predominantly black city of Ferguson, which ultimately led to several days of rioting. The St. Louis County Grand Jury did not indict Officer Wilson and more rioting ensued in Ferguson. Because of complaints from Ferguson residents about the Ferguson police department, the Department of Justice opened an investigation and found that some Ferguson police officers had routinely violated the constitutional rights of many of its African American residents.

Michael Brown's death reopened wounds from my childhood, reminding me that I was still black and powerless within a white society. As I watched the events unfold on television, I felt as if physical violence could be done to me, my son, my wife, or my daughter at any time and nothing would be done about it because we were black.

It reminded me of the time when I was sixteen and was pulled over for speeding. I was going 42mph in a 35mph zone. The white police officer approached the car and said, "Get out of the car and stand right over there on the sidewalk and don't move." I did what I was told while the police officer called for backup. Once his backup arrived, another white police officer came and stood right next to me, while the first officer began to search my car.

With a flashlight in his hand, he checked under the driver and passenger seats. He then checked the glove box, the back seat, and under the car. As a sixteen year old, African American teenager, I felt helpless and scared. I felt humiliated as drivers continued to pass by and stare. I wondered to myself, "Did he have the right to search my car? Did he follow police protocol when he pulled me over? Why was he treating me this way? I am a good kid!" As these questions and many others filled my mind, I ultimately realized that he could do to me whatever he wanted, and that saddened me. Just as the situation of Michael Brown's death had.

Emotional Isolation

So what was I feeling on that Sunday morning in August of 2014? I felt a sort of isolation, a form of mental and emotional alienation, from my white brothers and sisters. But they were unaware of it. The death of Michael Brown was an American tragedy, a tragedy that seemed all too familiar to me as a black man living in America. I felt pain, anger, and extreme sadness and there was no way that I could separate myself from the events that occurred.

I felt isolated from my white brothers and sisters because not many of them, if any, knew the regular pain, disappointment, discouragement, resentment, and anger I regularly worked through as a black man in a white world—as a black man in their white world.

For example, I often talk with a certain inflection and tone in my voice when I speak to white people in order not to communicate that I am uneducated, criminal, or a thug. I also have to be very aware of my facial expressions, posture, and demeanor in order not to bring fear to whites or make them think I am an "angry black man." I navigate a world of whites where little from my African American culture is valued or embraced, particularly in the church.

It is also difficult to overhear comments from my white brothers and sisters which reveal their negative bias towards African Americans—as poor, criminal, lazy, uneducated, and thuggish. It seems that many of my white brothers and sisters fail to see blacks, particularly poor blacks, as people made in the image and likeness of God, and thus their human equals.

As a result, I felt isolated, alienated, and emotionally distant that Sunday morning because my fellow church members—white church members—did not know their black brother's experience with racism in America.

A Racialized Society

There is a divide that still exists today between white and black Christians in America. Dr. Martin Luther King Jr. once said, "It is appalling that the most segregated hour of Christian America is eleven o'clock on Sunday morning."[1] In my mind, I like to believe that things have changed a little since Dr. King made that statement. Today we see more multi-ethnic churches in America than ever before. It is not uncommon today to visit suburban churches, in predominantly white affluent neighborhoods, and see at least a few African Americans, Hispanics, or Koreans. However, about 90 percent of African Americans attend predominantly black congregations and at least 95 percent of white Americans, and probably higher, attend predominantly white churches.[2] Why? I believe the true divide between white and black Christians comes from the way they view and experience racism within American society. George A. Yancey, author of *Beyond Racial Gridlock*, put it this way: "Perhaps the most important distinction between people of different races is the way we understand the concept of racism."[3]

Although white and black Christians can attend the same churches, work together at the same job, shop at the same stores, and live in the same neighborhoods, each can have drastically different experiences as American citizens. During the Ferguson unrest in August of 2014, my pastor, Scott Hickox, asked if I would help him and the church elders gain a different perspective on the riots that were going on in Ferguson. At the time, we had six elders and I was the only black elder at our church, which was a predominantly white suburban church in St. Louis. The first thought that came to my mind was my then, fifteen-year-old son Caleb. He was about 5'10" with a slim athletic build and long dreadlocks. With anger, pain, and resentment in my heart I said,

[1] King, Martin Luther. *Meet The Press* (Lawrence E. Spivak). Washington D.C. Television. April 17, 1960.

[2] Emerson, Michael O. and Smith, Christian, *Divided by Faith* (New York: Oxford University Press, 2001), p. 16.

[3] Yancey, George, *Beyond Racial Gridlock* (Downers Grove, IL: Intervarsity Press, 2006), pp. 11-12.

"I have had three conversations already with my son about how to present himself as a safe black man if he is ever pulled over by a cop, and I am angry that I have to have yet another conversation with him!" With tears in my eyes I continued. "You all will never have to have that conversation with your sons!"

As I sat there weeping, my pastor quietly responded, "You are right, I will never have to have that conversation with my sons, and I'm sorry." The rest of the elders were shocked; they wondered how anyone could possibly see my kind and gentle son as a threat. But I understood something that they did not. I knew, from experience, that if my son was not dressed right, if he did not talk right, if he looked like he was out of place in a predominantly white area or neighborhood, some police officer might see him as a criminal, a thug, and a threat.

We live in a racialized society. In his book, *Divided by Faith*, Michael Emerson defines a racialized society as "a society wherein race matters profoundly for differences in life experiences, life opportunities, and social relationships."[1] Sociologist Edward Bonilla-Silva defines such a racialized society as "a society that allocates differential economic, political, social and even psychological rewards to groups along racial lines, lines that are socially constructed."[2]

To many white Christians, the idea of a racialized society in 2017 is hard to comprehend. They might argue that the same opportunity exists in America for anyone who is willing to work hard. This statement has some truth to it, but if a person asked many black Christians if they thought we live in a racialized society, they may look at that person with a curious smile and say, "Uh, you're kidding, right? Of course we live in a racialized society. You don't see it?"

For many black Christians, racism is an ever-present reality that is woven into the fabric of American society. It affects government, law, education, housing, income, resources, employment, incarceration, and more. The racism that many black Christians refer to may not be the form of racism from

---

[1] Emerson and Smith, *Divided by Faith*, p. 7.

[2] Bonilla-Silva, Edward, "Rethinking Racism: Toward a Structural Interpretation." American Sociological Review 62, no. 3 (June 1997): pp. 465-480.

the past, what some would call "historical racism." This type of racism insisted that blacks were savage, inferior, and sub-human. This form of racism also made slavery, segregation, and Jim Crow laws possible. But the racism that many black Americans cite today is sometimes referred to as "structural" or "systemic" racism. In his book, *Portraits of White Racism*, David Wellman defines racism as "a system of advantage based on race."[1] Beverly Tatum, a clinical psychologist, author, and educator says, "This definition is useful because it allows us to see that racism, like other forms of oppression, is not only a personal ideology based on racial prejudice, but a system involving cultural messages and institutional policies and practices as well as the beliefs and actions of individuals. In the context of the United States, this system clearly operates to the advantage of Whites and to the disadvantage of people of color."[2]

In his book, *The End of White Christian America*, Robert P. Jones does a great job highlighting how this system of advantage based on race, works against black Americans:

> ". . . public opinion data show that there has been little progress in closing this racial perception gap over the past two decades. In 1992, the same year that the riots exploded in Los Angeles following the beating of Rodney King, an unarmed black taxi driver, by a group of white police officers, fewer than one in ten (8 percent) black Americans reported that they believed blacks and other minorities were treated the same as whites in the criminal justice system, while 89 percent disagreed. White Americans, by contrast, were almost evenly divided over whether blacks and whites received equal treatment in the criminal justice (46 percent agreed while 43 percent disagreed). More than two decades later, the racial perception gap stands at more than 30 percentage points: only 14 percent of black Americans, compared to 47 percent of white Americans, agree that the criminal

[1] Wellman, David T., *Portraits of White Racism*, (New York: Cambridge University Press, 1993), p. 104.

[2] Tatum, Beverly Daniel, *Why are All the Black Kids Sitting Together in the Cafeteria?* (New York: Basic Books, 1997), p. 25.

[3] Jones, Robert P., *The End of White Christian America* (New York: Simon and Schuster, 2016), pp. 152-153.

20

justice system treats minorities the same as whites."[3]

Emotional Distance

Because of these differing points of view, and the experience of racism for black Christians, there is a certain emotional distance that exists between white and black Christians. This emotional distance is not easy to detect for white Christians because most black Christians—who spend most of their time in predominantly white settings (work, church, school, etc.)—have learned to assimilate well; so well, in fact, their white co-worker, church member or friend, may never know just how drastically racism affects them. If their black friends do not share these experiences with them, they may never know. The experience of racism for many black Christians can create an emotional and psychological distance between them and their white Christian brothers and sisters. This distance may be hard to overcome. Not because their white Christian friends are racists, but because their white Christian friends are often unaware of the deep emotional and psychological pain they have experienced due to racism. The unfortunate part is that it may have never occurred to their white Christian friends that their black Christian friends have ever experienced any sort of racism. However, ignorance does not close the emotional distance between them. Ironically, some black Christians may not consciously be aware of the distance either. Many of them have just learned to operate within predominantly white communities without ever discussing personal incidents of racism with their white Christian friends.

I remember talking to two African American students a few years ago. When I asked them if any of their white classmates had ever said anything racially insensitive, one of the African American students said, "Yes" and the other said "No." The student who answered, "Yes" cited a few examples. In response to hearing the examples, the black student, who had originally said "No," then said, "Oh, yeah, that type of stuff does happen, but I am so used to it that I don't even notice it anymore." This student had learned to cope with situations and comments that were racially insensitive, so much so, she did not even notice them anymore. Because she had learned to ignore these comments, most likely she also ignored the feelings associated with the comments. Those feelings are what could create emotional distance between her and her white friends.

Sometimes black Christians who have close white Christians friends and spend a lot of time in settings that are predominantly white, prefer not to talk about race because it makes them feel uncomfortable. It makes them stand out from their white Christians friends and they don't want that. Also, they may have great love and admiration for their white Christians friends, and they do not want them to feel uncomfortable about the subject of race, so they try to stay away from those conversations.

There are other black Christians who may have never really thought much about their experiences with racism. There are many reasons for this, but sometimes it is because they were not raised in a community that is predominantly black, but spent most of their life in communities that are predominantly white. This could affect how they view racism. In some cases, they may not agree racism is a major problem. Someone may ask them about racism and they may not have much to say. However, they would probably acknowledge that the experience of black people as a whole in America society is different from that of whites.

A Wide Divide

Black Christians, who are part of a predominantly black or multi-ethnic church, or reside in an urban neighborhood, may be more aware of racial inequality between whites and blacks than those who do not. This may particularly be true if they live in a lower income neighborhood and have worked in jobs where they are in the minority. The reality of driving every day from where they live to a job in a more affluent part of town can be a constant reminder of the racial and socioeconomic disparity that often exists in cities across America.

When I was a kid in the mid to late 70's, we moved from the inner city to the suburbs. However, most of our extended family still lived in the city, and our home church was in the city as well. The neighborhood we moved into was a predominantly white, middle-class, working-class, neighborhood. We were one of the first black families to move into the neighborhood. Because of our extended family and our church, we often spent the weekdays in the suburbs and the weekends in the city. One of my most vivid memories as a boy was watching the neighborhoods change from good neighborhoods to bad neighborhoods as we drove from the suburbs to the city.

In my mind, the suburbs were neat, clean, and peaceful. There were beautiful parks, great restaurants, public and private schools. There were jobs, resources, libraries, grocery stores, shopping malls, and baseball fields. In the city, there was trash left in the streets, dilapidated buildings, liquor stores, abandoned buildings, and houses that no one came to fix. There was violence, crime, poverty, frustration, failing public schools, lack of jobs, lack of resources, lack of hope, and a great sense of hopelessness that anything would change for those who could not afford to move out. As a child, even I could see the disparity; I just did not understand it. From my vantage point it seemed as if white people had all the advantages in life.

As I grew older, I came to understand that not all white people lived a life of luxury, but I perceived there was still something different about my experience and that of my white friends who lived in the same neighborhood as I and whose parents earned just a little more than mine. The difference was race. The color of my black skin could not be hidden; it was often a liability for me in my interactions with white teachers, parents, neighbors, store clerks, classmates—consciously and unconsciously. However, for my white friends whose family's financial situation was as dire as mine, they did not encounter the same social challenges as I did. Over the years, I have witnessed and experienced the social and psychological experiences tied to race and have found, for myself and many blacks in America, it is extremely different from that of whites. The memories of these experiences for blacks are often filled with pain, resentment, and bitterness.

These experiences are personal; they often are not shared with white Christians for fear that they will try to explain away the experience as anything other than racism. For example, there have been times when I have shared with white Christian friends about my experiences of being stopped by a white police officer. They immediately told me about a time when they, or some other white person they knew, were pulled over by a white police officer. I assume they said this in order to prove that the police officers did not have racial bias but were simply doing their jobs. Could their statement be true? Absolutely. However, I am always curious why their first response was to defend the police officer and try to prove the police treated them in the same manner and without racial bias. I have had this conversation so many times with my white Christian friends that as soon as they provide multiple examples of why their interaction with a police officer is just like mine, I usually just listen intently, allow them to finish, and then concede the argument to them.

You might ask, "So Aaron, what would you desire in this situation?" As a black Christian, I simply want my white Christian friends to listen to me share my experience and consider what is often hard to admit: Racism and racial bias in America is still an issue. I am not asking you to agree with every instance that blacks claim racism. I only ask you to consider: Is racism plausible in this case? I am asking my white brothers and sisters to challenge their own thinking concerning racism and inequality in America.

Here is how you can practice challenging yourself: When you hear of a situation on television, radio, social media, or elsewhere claiming racism or racial discrimination, play "devil's advocate" with yourself. Refute all of your initial knee-jerk reactions and thoughts, and challenge each one with an opposing argument. Start off by saying things like this, "Maybe there is an incident of racism here?" or "Maybe they are treating blacks unfairly?" or "I wonder if the person was white would they have been treated in such an awful way?" I am challenging you to think this way because I think it is helpful, and it can produce a certain degree of empathy that may be hard to obtain otherwise. I can testify this type of practice is helpful because I have done it for years.

Let me concede that I am not immune to racial bias; none of us are. We all suffer the effects of media driven stereotypes and biases, but it is helpful if we are aware of our own biases. Because I am aware of my biases, I challenge them. For example, when

I initially heard about the Michael Brown shooting, I was very emotional about it. It was easy, too easy, for me to simply blame Officer Wilson. But I chose to challenge my own thinking and my own biases. This was helpful. This allowed me not to demonize Officer Wilson and place all of the responsibility on him. It also allowed me not to ignore the complexity of the interaction between Officer Wilson and Michael Brown. It allowed me to explore how policemen are trained to deal with civilian conflicts, and although I do believe a degree of racial bias was a factor in the Michael Brown shooting, challenging my own biases was incredibly helpful in gaining another perspective and keeping my heart from becoming bitter. I believe we should all challenge our biases whenever we are aware of them.

If white Christians are unaware of their unconscious racial bias, it can lead to extreme emotional pain and isolation for their black brothers and sisters. I remember one night when I was in high school and a group of my classmates and I were coming home from a professional baseball game that had gone into extra innings and did not end until after twelve o'clock in the morning. We were all part of a local Fellowship of Christian Athletes group at our high school. There were five of us in the car—four were white—and I was the only black person in the car. We were stopped by a police officer because our driver made an illegal left-hand turn. The policeman approached the car and asked for the license and registration of the young lady who was driving. He began to explain to her what an illegal left-hand turn was and then he asked her, "Where are you coming from?" She explained we were a group of students coming back from a baseball game. The policeman then pointed his flashlight in the car. He pointed it at me and said, "How old are you, son?" I replied, "Fifteen." He responded, "Do you know that you are out after curfew?" I then answered, "I did not know that there was a curfew." The policeman did not ask anyone else in the car how old they were. He then went back to his car, wrote me a ticket and said, "Give this ticket to your dad." The policeman then turned to the driver and continued to explain to her what she did wrong. He eventually let her off without giving her a ticket.

We rode home in silence. As each of my friends got out of the car at their respective homes, I desperately wanted at least one of them to say, "The way the police officer treated you was unfair. He did not ask us our ages, and he did not even give a ticket to the person driving, or explain why he had stopped us." But none of them said anything but goodbye and walked up to their houses. I was the last one to be dropped off. The driver and I rode in awkward silence as we approached my house. I thought for sure she was waiting for our other friends to get out of the car to say something to me. She would apologize right? She would say the officer had been unfair? I thought to myself, "Of course she will say something. She was the oldest and it was her actions that led to us being pulled over." But as we stopped in front of my house, we both said our goodbyes. I got out of the car with the pink ticket in my hand and closed the car door. As she drove away, I stood in my driveway looking at the ticket and realizing that my white Christian friends had failed me. They allowed me to suffer in silence.

1 Corinthians 12:24-25 says, "But God has so composed the body, giving greater honor to the part that lacked it, that there may be no division in the body, but that the members may have the same care for one another. If one member suffers, all suffer together." In this chapter of 1 Corinthians, the Apostle Paul addresses the church at Corinth about spiritual gifts within the body of Christ. Paul goes on to say there are a variety of different gifts within the body and none of the spiritual gifts are without value. As Paul moves further through the chapter, his thoughts about spiritual gifts parallel his thoughts about the "members" of the body. The members of the body are also known as Christians. Just as there are a variety of spiritual gifts, and all are valuable, so also are there many members in the body of Christ and all of them are valuable.

Later in the chapter, Paul establishes that the "members," though different, are a part of one and the same body. The members are united in one body; they are not divided. Paul maintains that each member needs the other and no member should look down on another member; rather, each should honor the other. Paul gives a practical application for unity among the members in verse 25, saying, "that there may be no division in the body, but that the members may have the same care for one another." This means that members should not think of other members in ways that communicate they are not a member of the body; that would be a form of division. Paul goes a step further by saying that each member should have the same care for each and every member. He is saying that all members should be treated and cared for in the same way, because they are members of the body. Paul highlights the depth of the unity among the members adding, "If one member suffers, all suffer together . . ." (v. 26).

As members of the same body, we are to suffer together. When I walked up my driveway toward my house that night, with the police ticket in my hand, I did not feel as though my white Christian friends had suffered with me. What did I expect from them? Did I expect them to stand up and challenge the policeman? No, I just would have liked for them to acknowledge that something unjust had occurred. The hardest pill to swallow that night was that none of my white Christian friends condemned the policeman's actions. Situations like these, for black Christians, can create emotional distance between them and their white Christian friends.

Closing the Distance

What is at the core of the emotional distance? The distance is present because for many black Christians, the reality of racism, or the psychological effects of it are very personal. It is very difficult to be deeply connected to someone who does not know, or who may not empathize with, your past and present experiences with racism.

It is very challenging for black Christians to witness the silence from white Christians on unjust violent crimes against people of color. Many black Christians wonder why more white Christians do not speak out against these crimes. Why don't they challenge a crime that could be racially motivated?

When I ask these types of questions, I sometimes get "push back" from my white Christian friends who ask me, "What about black on black crime?" This is a good and fair question. I respond by saying, "There is black on black crime, and I will never look past that." In fact, when I was a teacher in the Ferguson-Florissant school district, I constantly challenged my black students to follow the law, to be good citizens, and not to further negative stereotypes about blacks. I support holding young black men and women accountable for their actions and giving them the support and opportunities they need to be productive, law-abiding citizens. But the fact that black on black crime exists does not negate the fact that we should all challenge injustices towards blacks.

I am not advocating for white Christians to pacify black Christians on every occasion by siding with blacks in every proclaimed racial injustice. Rather, I am just reiterating that white Christians have to be willing to challenge their own cultural biases. We all have cultural and racial bias and we should always ask ourselves good questions and be courageous enough to say, when it seems to be true, "This was not right!" This type of thoughtful action can help close some of the emotional distance between white and black Christians.

A few years ago, my white friend and co-worker, Dave, helped me close the emotional gap between us with two courageous racial conversations he initiated. The first conversation took place after Dave and I were reunited as teachers working at a Christian school in St. Louis. (Ten years earlier, Dave and I had worked together at public high school). After working together for several months, Dave and I were in the weight room and he asked me, "What is it like being one of the few black teachers working here?" At that time, there were only three black teachers on a staff of about 130. Dave's question caught me totally by surprise; I was speechless. After a few seconds I looked at Dave and said, "You know what? No one has ever asked me that."

In that moment, something happened between Dave and me; I immediately felt a little closer to him. Dave had taken a step toward me, into my experience as a black man working in a predominantly white work place. Dave's curiosity allowed me to share my experience with him and it brought us closer.

The second conversation took place probably a year or so

later, after Dave and his wife had gone to see the movie, *The Help*. After seeing the movie, Dave seemed a little troubled by the fact that many of the white characters in the movie seemed okay with the way the black maids—the help—were treated. This caused Dave to question whether he would have behaved any differently had he lived during that time. When Dave saw me a few days later and told me he had seen the movie, I asked him what he thought. He paused and said, "I keep asking myself, 'If I had been alive back then, would I have done something about the way the black maids were treated?' And I have come to the conclusion that I may not have."

I was intrigued by Dave's comment. First, I could tell he had spent considerable time thinking about it. Second, I was struck by his honesty. Why did he feel the need to share this with me? Why was there remorse in his voice when he confessed he would not have responded any differently than the white characters in the movie who had upheld the status quo? Dave was feeling empathy for the black maids in the movie and he was feeling empathy for me. In that moment, I would have shared anything with Dave about my experience as a black man. He made me feel safe to share. He also made me think that he would listen to me because he expressed a desire to learn. I did not feel as though Dave wanted to argue with me; I felt like Dave wanted to learn from me and wanted to help me in some way. Needless to say, Dave is one of my closest friends and we have regular conversations about issues of race, racism, and injustice. He had courage to lean into a potentially difficult conversation with me, his black Christian friend, and both of us are better because of it. These two conversations began to close the emotional distance between us.

It is important to note the emotional distance that exists between white and black Christians goes both ways. It is not only an emotional distance that black Christians experience towards white Christians. I believe it can occur from white Christians towards black Christians also. If my white brother or sister has had a bad experience with blacks, such as being called a name or experiencing a hostile encounter with someone black, it could cause emotional distance for white Christians towards black Christians. For instance, another one of my white colleagues, Lara, shared with me that when she first moved to St. Louis from Texas, she and her sister had a bad encounter with a black student. During their first interaction with a black student, the student referred to Lara's sister as a "rich, white, b****!" Lara stood there with an incredulous look on her face and began to cry. She could not understand why this student would say such a thing.

This experience, I believe to some degree, and understandably so, left a mark in Lara's mind about African Americans. What had Lara's sister done? What reason did the student have to lash out at her sister? Lara's experience created some emotional distance. Lara did not share this story with me when we initially became colleagues, but it was after several years of working together, and after several open conversations about race. At some point early in our conversations about race, Lara probably thought about her first encounter with the black student and wondered what I would think about it, and whether I could sympathize and empathize with her. I believe she experienced the emotional divide as well. But when I listened to the story of her experience, I closed some of the emotional distance between us.

There is a divide, an emotional distance that exists between white and black Christians, and the divide is a product of living within a racialized society. Although white and black Christians can live in the same neighborhoods, shop at the same stores, work for the same companies, go to the same schools, and attend the same churches, their experiences, based upon their race, can still be drastically different. If we are to close the emotional distance between white and black Christians, we must create space for intentional conversations.

Discussion Questions

1. Why does emotional distance exist between white and black Christians?

2. Why do you think black Christians tend to be more aware of the emotional distance than white Christians?

3. What are some things that increase the emotional distance between black and white Christians?

4. Why are white Christians often silent when there are violent crimes committed against blacks?

5. How did Dave close some of the emotional distance between himself and Aaron?

6. What are some ways white Christians can begin to close the emotional distance between themselves and black Christians?

2

The American-Racial Paradigm

"Whites were the winners, blacks were the losers, we wrote the
history books, and they didn't feature."
—Philip Noyce

It was well after 10:00 p.m. on election night of 2008. I sat with
my mother-in-law, father-in-law, uncle, and my wife to watch
the election results. We watched with disbelief and amazement
as the final vote counts scrolled across the television screen.
There was silence in the room as we all sat transfixed in front of
the television. I thought to myself, "What just happened? Did
America just elect the first black president?"

Before the night began, this seemed improbable to me. As I
tried to gather my thoughts about what the election results meant,
my mother-in-law broke the silence, and blurted out in a loud
voice, "Y'all don't know how it was for us! Y'all don't know how it
was for us!" I was taken aback by her tone because she was usually
a very mild and meek woman, but somehow she had gained the
strength to speak her mind.

She had our attention and continued, "I remember being
a little girl in Mississippi, and I remember how it was for us. I
remember segregation. I lived through segregation!" She stared at
the television screen and recounted a painful childhood memory.
"I remember one time my aunt and I were taking a bus to a
department store. When we got on the bus, I was excited because
the bus was empty and I thought to myself, 'I can sit wherever I

33

want.' But as I picked out a seat and sat in it, my aunt instructed me to get up and go to the back of the bus. I did not understand why I could not sit there. My aunt then told me that those seats were for whites."

After she finished the story, my mother-in-law turned to us and said, "I didn't think I would ever see the day that America would have a black president." Why was my mother-in-law surprised? Why were we surprised? And why were African Americans all over the country crying and celebrating? Were they celebrating Barak Obama's policies? In truth, many black Americans were celebrating the simple fact that Barak Obama was black and he had won the presidency. This was a victory that reached back into the past, into the time of segregation and farther back into slavery. It was a victory for all blacks—past, present, and future. For many blacks, it was not political at all. The victory loomed large for black Americans for one main reason: It challenged the historic vantage point of whites over blacks within American society.

Subordinate Position

A paradigm can be defined as an example, pattern, or worldview about a subject. In America's troubled racial past, there was a racial paradigm about whites and blacks that prevailed for many years. This paradigm was born out of the initial relationship between whites and blacks in the early years of our country's formation. Many say that the first Africans to come to America arrived in Jamestown, Virginia in 1619. There were about twenty of them in a cargo-hold of a Dutch ship, whom the captain and his crew had stolen from a Spanish ship. It is unclear whether the Africans were slaves or indentured servants, but by 1640 the institution of American slavery had begun.

The relationship between whites and blacks in the early founding of America was filled with tension from the start. White Americans were largely in the dominant role and held the superior position within American society, and black Americans were in the subordinate position. For most of America's young history, this has been the social hierarchy. When we talk about the changes and advancements for blacks within American society, these changes are still fairly recent. If we consider Jamestown, Virginia as the first permanent English settlement in America in 1607 and count forward to 2016, America is 409 years old. It has only been in the last 50 years or so that blacks have, by law and practice, become equal citizens. This is not to say that we have not made progress in race relations and opportunities for blacks, but if we take a step back and look at the big picture of American race relations, we see there is much in our past to overcome. And yes, as white and black Christians, we both believe that Jesus is the answer and the gospel is the key to true racial reconciliation. At the same time, there have been many Americans throughout America's history, who loved Jesus, preached the gospel, and evangelized the four corners of America, yet somehow still believed the social hierarchy that allowed for slavery and segregation was somehow ordained by God.

Emerson makes the point in *Divided by Faith* that many Christians did not believe it was part of their responsibility to speak out against the injustice of slavery. He says:

"Efforts to evangelize, we have seen, led Christians to support the wider racialized status quo. To challenge the very foundations of the larger system was simply not part of their worldview. Further, as Berger, among others, notes, the connection between cultural and religious legitimation is often strong. To overturn slavery was seen as going against God's ordained pattern." Robert P. Jones, the author of, The End of White Christian America, put it this way, ". . . White Christian America has not been without its critics and controversies. Its reputation was especially marred by its general accommodation to and participation in the institution of slavery up until the Civil War. In the late nineteenth and twentieth centuries, White Christian America's apathy toward-and in some quarters even staunch defense of-segregation in the American South did little to overturn these negative associations."[1]

This highlights that what I call the *American-Racial Paradigm* was deeply rooted in the American psyche. And for some white

---

[1] Emerson and Smith, *Divided by Faith*, p. 18.

Christians, not even their love and devotion to Jesus and their belief in the gospel overturned their minds and led them to act against the evils of slavery.

A Heart Problem

So what are you saying, Brother Layton? Are you saying Jesus and the gospel are not the answer to racial reconciliation between whites and blacks in America? No, I am not saying that. Jesus and the gospel are the only real, sustainable hope for racial reconciliation and any true reconciliation among humans. If Jesus reconciled us to the Father (Rom. 5:10) then he is more than able to reconcile white and black Christians. The problem is not with Jesus; it is with our hearts. As the famous line of the hymn "Come Thou Fount of Every Blessing" reads, ". . . prone to wander Lord I feel it, prone to leave the God I love." Our hearts wander from the Lord in varying degrees and often we are not aware that we are turning toward idols.

How could God-fearing, Christ-loving, Spirit-led Christians support a social hierarchy that in practice was not consistent with all men being valued because they are God's image-bearers? Genesis 1:26 says, "Then God said, 'Let us make man in our image, after our likeness.'" This passage reveals the distinction and dignity for all of mankind. Man bears the image of God and therefore man has inherent value and worth. In Genesis 9:6, God reiterates this point by saying, "Whoever sheds the blood of man, by man shall his blood be shed, for God made man in his own image." God says that the value of human life is directly connected to humans being made in God's image and likeness. The life of a man is so valuable that if an animal takes a man's life then the animal must die (9:5), and if one man takes the life of another man then that man should die. Of all the creatures on the earth, man is the most valuable and his existence should demand the value God assigned to it. Ironically, the founders of our country got it right in their proclamation, "We hold these truths to be self-evident, that all men are created equal, that they are endowed by their Creator with certain unalienable rights . . ." but they got it wrong in their practice towards African Americans,

Native Americans, and other ethnic minorities.

So how could God-fearing, Christ-loving, Spirit-led Christians support a social hierarchy that is clearly inconsistent with the way Christ followers are called to act towards one another? The answer is: idols. Such idols might have been power, money, resources, a way of life, control, prestige, pride, or ethnic supremacy. Whenever members of a group have something to protect or something they are afraid they could lose, it can become an idol. For example, many white Christians in the South during slavery and Jim Crow supported the social hierarchy because of economics. The social structure of the day was more advantageous to their way of life. The livelihood of many Southern Christians was connected to the institution of slavery. This economic idol caused their hearts to wander in such a way that many Southern Christians defended slavery, did not oppose it, or did not speak out against it. Interestingly enough, Northern white Christians were not necessarily nobler than their Southern brothers and sisters; they had the luxury of not having their standard of living tied up in slave labor. It has now been many years since the institution of slavery was firmly rooted within the American society, and although slavery has long since been abolished, there still remains societal idols of our racial past that continue to affect the way white and black Christians view and interact with one another.

Racial Bias

If we are honest with ourselves—and we need to be or else we will not change—black Christians may unconsciously have racial bias towards whites and white Christians may unconsciously have racial bias towards blacks. Maybe both white and black Christians, though it may be hard, can to some degree admit that. If we can admit that, I believe we are laying a great foundation for true and lasting racial reconciliation.

Often when I am engaged with one of my white Christian friends in a conversation about race, I can sense their nervousness and fear. They seem to be afraid that they may say something unknowingly that is racially offensive. I usually try to put them at ease because I recognize that it is not always easy to have a conversation about race with someone who is black and I want to validate their courage and encourage them to continue with the conversation. But why is it so hard for white Christians to admit to having racial biases? I believe that some white Christians fear that if they admit to some racial biases, they will be judged holistically as racist and/or evil.

First of all, just because a person has some racial biases, it does not mean they are a racist: they could just be lacking in cultural understanding and suffering from media bias. For example, when I was fourteen, a Puerto Rican family of four moved into our neighborhood. The son's name was Abnel and he was just a year older than me. We became friends because we both played football and both walked to school. Prior to meeting the Ortiz family, the only information I had about Puerto Ricans had come from television. My lone view of Puerto Ricans came from Juan Epstein, a character in the hit 70's television series called, "Welcome Back Kotter." Needless to say, my limited view of Puerto Ricans was filled with pejorative stereotypes. So it came as a complete surprise to me when Abnel told me his father was an aeronautical engineer for McDonnell Douglas, which later became Boeing. Was I racist because I never thought there could be a Puerto Rican aeronautical engineer? Or was I just biased based upon my limited interactions and knowledge of Puerto Rican people and culture? I was not racist, but I was racially biased.

I recognize that there may be a real fear for white Christians to explore their racial biases and lean into these conversations, but I want to encourage you to be courageous and honest with your black Christian friends. I think most black Christians would welcome and appreciate the effort and humility from their white brothers and sisters to admit some of their racial biases.

There is another challenge I see among Christians that impedes the progress of uncovering racial bias. It is the idea that because we are Christian, we are somehow immune to racial bias. Let me concede this point for all of us as Christians: we all have racial bias to some degree. Only God, Jesus, and the Holy

Spirit have absolutely no racial biases. Do you know what having racial biases means for you and me? It means we are human, humans affected by the fallen world we live in. Just think about it for a moment, from the time you and I were children, we have been bombarded with images, sound bites, videos, movies, books, magazines, television shows, newspapers, friends, parents, teachers, professors and now social media, all presenting material that has a direct impact on us and our thinking. To some degree, we cannot avoid all societal influences; however, we can and must be aware of them. This can help us challenge and resist some of our racial biases that are not founded on personal experiences, but may have been introduced to us through the media and other sources.

Here is a helpful exercise I often use to challenge my racial biases and/or racial stereotypes. I ask myself a few simple questions like: "Aaron is that true because of your personal experience with that person/people group or because you have heard it or seen it somewhere and it seemed true? And if you do know that to be true about that person/people group, is it possible this may not be true for others or all the people in that group?" It is amazing what this simple exercise can do for identifying racial biases and deconstructing them. Every one of us is prone to racial biases and as Christians we can't think we are immune to the influences of our culture. Instead, we should become aware of our racial biases and work against them.

A New Ethnos

As Christians, we have help in this. Christ has laid the only foundation in the universe that can withstand racial, ethnic, and cultural divisions. The Apostle Paul's words in Ephesians 2:11-19 inform us on how Christ laid the foundation for cultural and ethnic unity between Jews and Gentiles:

> "Therefore remember that at one time you Gentiles in the flesh, called "the uncircumcision" by what is called the circumcision, which is made in the flesh by hands, remember that you were at that time separated from Christ, alienated from the commonwealth of Israel and

strangers to the covenants of promise, having no hope and without God in the world. But now in Christ Jesus you who were far off have been brought near by the blood of Christ. For he himself is our peace, who has made us both one and has broken down in his flesh the dividing wall of hostility by abolishing the law of commandments expressed in ordinances, that he might create in himself one new man in place of the two, so making peace, and might reconcile us both to God in one body through the cross, thereby killing the hostility . . . so then you are no longer strangers and aliens, but you are fellow citizens with saints and members of the household of God."

The Jews were the ethnic group that was "the circumcised" and for the Jew, circumcision represented God's covenant, his promises, his faithfulness, and his devotion to them. The Gentiles on the other hand were "the uncircumcised." They were outside God's covenant, his promises, and his devotion. A Gentile was anyone from any ethnic group that was not a Jew. Jews and Gentiles were two separate cultural groups. Jewish culture was inextricably connected to God, his laws and commandments; the culture of the Gentiles was not connected to God, his laws, and his commandments. The Gentiles lived under other cultural practices, many of which were condemned by the God of the Jews.

The initial division between Jew and Gentile was religious, but later it became more. When Jews referred to Gentiles as "the uncircumcised," it was often to ridicule or mock them. In 1 Samuel 17:26, David stood before King Saul and the armies of Israel. He was beside himself with anger as the Philistine giant, Goliath, taunted the Israelite armies. When David asked the king what reward there would be for killing Goliath, he referred to him as the "uncircumcised" Philistine. For the Jew, circumcision was a big deal and it was serious enough to keep Jews separated from Gentiles.

But Christ, by providing atonement for the Gentiles through his blood, has brought them near to God. Now the old distinctions, or divisions of Jew and Gentile, have been destroyed, along with any hostility, because Christ has died for all and all have access to God through Christ. Christ unites the two ethnic groups into one. How does he do that? He creates a new spiritual ethnicity. For all who are in Christ, past, present, and future, have become part of this new ethnos. There is no longer division between Jew and Gentile believers; the Jews and Gentiles have been brought together by Christ—not only Jews and Gentiles but all ethnic Christians. He has united us all in himself. Paul says it this way in verse 15, "that he might create in himself one new man in place of the two . . . " Christ has united all ethnic believers into one body and created peace between them. A better way of saying this is: Christ has united us and laid a foundation for peace between us. But we must continually work towards that peace.

We must be careful not to misinterpret what it means for believers to be part of this new ethnos. It does not mean we should ignore our ethnic (black, white, etc.) differences, for God created us that way and our ethnicity is part of the beauty of God's diverse world. We only need to recognize our most important ethnicity, which is Christian, and we must work to not have bias towards our brother's and sister's earthly ethnicity. We can see a glimpse of what that new ethnos looks like when we read Revelation 7:9. "After this I looked, and behold, a great multitude that no one could number, from every nation, from all tribes, and peoples and languages, standing before the throne and before the Lamb."

The new ethnos is not a group in which we do not see or acknowledge ethnic distinctions, but a group that does not allow those distinctions to divide us. If we can acknowledge our racial biases to one another, in an atmosphere of love and humility, we can begin to overcome them.

Us vs. Them

The American-Racial Paradigm is simply what I call an "us versus them" mentality. I believe it has prevailed, consciously and unconsciously, within American society since our early years as a nation. At the core of this paradigm is the notion that the whites in American society were against the blacks. As much as we would like to ignore this paradigm, it still challenges us today. Just think about it for a moment: whenever there is a high profile case and the opponents are white and black, we are tempted to retreat to our respective corners.

I cannot think of a better example than the 1995 O. J. Simpson murder trial. OJ was on trial for the murder of his wife, Nicole Brown, and her friend, Ronald Goldman. Nicole and Ronald were white and OJ was black. The nation was mesmerized by this case and it polarized black and white Americans. Blacks tended to support OJ and whites tended to support the prosecuting attorneys. Sadly, there were whites and blacks who had made up their minds about the case before the trial began and the evidence was revealed. We saw the same polarization in the Michael Brown shooting in Ferguson, Missouri in August of 2014. Blacks and whites both had retreated to their corners before there was any investigation.

Here is my question: Why do we do that? Why do many of us retreat to our racial corners when there is a racial controversy? Because woven into the fabric of American culture is the white versus black mentality. Since this mentality lies largely in our unconscious mind, it is difficult to identify. When we recognize this as part of American culture, we can work to deconstruct the thoughts that invade our minds. For example, as a black Christian who is not perfect and has a degree of racial bias, I might hear about the death of Michael Brown, prior to an investigation, and say, "Here is yet another case of a white police officer abusing his authority and killing another black male." But as a Christian, if I am aware of my racial bias and I am aware that I may be tempted to side with my race due to the black vs. white American paradigm, I can hit the brakes and say: 1) Christ destroyed ethnic divisions and I need to look beyond that. 2) I will not allow the American "Us versus Them" mentality to control my heart and assume the worst of the white police officer. 3) I will recognize who the real enemy is, the Devil; it is not the white person. Both black and white evangelical Christians can take this approach and it will help us to keep our hearts from becoming dark.

Paradigms can change, but because they usually are not

created overnight, they also do not change overnight. The American-Racial Paradigm for blacks and whites may linger in our unconscious minds, but if we pay attention to how we feel and what we think when there is racial conflict between whites and blacks, some of that paradigm will be exposed. If we are aware that we all have some degree of racial bias, and we can admit that bias to our black and white brothers and sisters in Christ who love us, we can begin to deconstruct the harmful and divisive American-Racial Paradigm. With regular intentional conversations, a church can create a rhythm of dialogue that can help shift the paradigm.

Discussion Questions

1. What is the "American-Racial Paradigm?" Do you believe it existed in American history? Do you believe that it exists today?

2. According to the text above, how did the American-Racial Paradigm became embedded into the conscience or subconscious mind of American society?

3. What lasting effects do you think 230 years of slavery and one hundred years of racial inequality have had on American society? List 4-5 effects.

4. Do you believe relationships between white and black Christians today are still hindered by our nation's past? If yes, in what way? If no, why not?

5. What are some strategies that could help to deconstruct the American-Racial Paradigm for white and black Christians?

3

Creating Space

"After Civil Rights, it was very awkward for whites and blacks.
We didn't know how to talk to each other."
—Nick Nolte

When I was a sophomore in high school, a tragedy occurred among our student body. One student stabbed another student at a party after a fight broke out. To this day, I am uncertain what exactly happened that night, but the student who was stabbed eventually died. It was the saddest day of my high school career, and one of the saddest days in my high school's history. The school community was stunned and grieved. Later, the student body would grow divided. Why? The student who stabbed the other student was black; the student stabbed was white.

Our school was like many other high schools in America. It was located in a predominantly white, middle class neighborhood. This produced a predominantly white student body. However, there were some African American students, some of whom lived in the area, and others were bussed in from other areas of the city. Although many, white and black, had gone to school together for several years, it was hard not to take sides along racial lines.

White students found reasons to blame the black student, and black students found reasons to blame the white student. I remember attending the funeral, which was held on a weekday during school hours. As I walked across the parking lot, I wondered if I should walk into the church with my white friends or with my black friends. Everything was so complicated. I don't think any of us, white or black, knew what to do or what to say to one another. I do remember there were school counselors available for students struggling with the student's death—but what about the racial tension? What about the growing racial divide? Who was going to address that?

In the end, no one would address it. We did not talk about it; we just went on with life. But what we needed was someone to create a safe space, a safe place, for us to talk about the tensions. We needed space and time to talk, but no one created that space for us. So we remained divided, not on the outside but on the inside.

Beginning Conversations

"We must provide space for conversations like this," said Greg Perry, a seminary professor at Covenant Theological Seminary in St. Louis, Missouri. He stood before an audience made up of predominantly black and white Christians. They had gathered for The City Ministry Conference in April 2015, held at Covenant Seminary. It was titled, "Welcoming One Another: Racial Identity in Christ." The conference was designed to create space to wrestle with how our personal stories and our racial and cultural identities are woven together in the larger identity of Christ's humanity. Here is the description of the conference from the seminary's website:

> We are confronted almost daily by bad news that dispels the myth of post-racial America. Is there any good news? How does the gospel weave our smaller personal stories and our racial and cultural identities into the larger identity of Christ's "one new humanity"? These are some of the questions we will explore together at this special conference sponsored by Covenant Seminary's City Ministry Initiative (CMI).[1]

Perry and the organizers for the conference understood that America is far from a post-racial society, but they also understood

[1] Covenant Seminary: The Thistle, "City Ministry Conference 2015: Welcoming One Another: Racial Identity in Christ" (blog post) March 11, 2015.

that many Christians had probably made the same assumption. If Christians made this assumption, then there was much to discuss. So what is at stake? What remains at stake is true unity within the ethnically diverse body of Christ.

Do They Care?

Michael Brown's death and the events of Ferguson revealed a significant racial divide between blacks and whites in America. These events not only revealed the racial divide, it also revealed the racial divide that exists between white and black Christians. Listening to conversations among white and black Christians during the time after Michael Brown's death, it was not hard to feel the divide. It was obvious from Facebook feeds and blog posts. Differing opinions on the Michael Brown case did not create the racial divide; it just revealed the divide that was underneath. For black Americans it was the result of past, personal, and often painful life experiences of being black in America.

Watching the chaos that ensued after the death of Michael Brown and the subsequent verdict, it appeared many white Christians did not understand the unrest in Ferguson. On the other hand, many black Christians, like myself, did not agree with nor condone the rioting, looting, and violence, but we understood the anger. We were angry too, but we chose to handle it differently. Many did not riot, many did not loot, and many did not use violence as a means to lash out. Instead, we tried not to let our emotions get the best of us. Then something interesting happened. Brown's death and the unrest in Ferguson caused many white Christians to ask, "What is going on here? Am I missing something?"

About a month after the death of Michael Brown, my heart was in turmoil. Most of my family and black friends were in constant conversation about Ferguson and systemic racism in St. Louis and across America. However, while I was at work or at church, both in predominantly white settings, my white colleagues, at least outwardly, did not seem too concerned about what was happening in Ferguson. I thought to myself, "How could they not care?" In my mind, to look at those black faces in Ferguson on

CNN was to look at me. These were my people. This feeling ate away at me on the inside until I finally decided to talk to a close white friend and colleague, Scott Holley. Scott and I had worked together for six years, and we had regular conversations about race. Scott had always been honest with me, and I needed him to be honest about this issue. I wanted to know what was going on in the minds of my white colleagues, friends, and church members.

One day after a faculty meeting, I turned to Scott and said, "Scott, do you think white Christians care about what is happening in Ferguson? And do they want to talk about it?" His answer caught me off guard. He said, "Aaron, I am white, and I was born and raised in a white neighborhood, and I understand that I have privileges because I am white. But here is the deal: We don't understand it. We don't know what to say. And we don't know what to do." Those three statements never occurred to me. I immediately came out of my funk, and I said to Scott, "If what you say is true, then we can address those problems with a little courage and a lot of dialogue."

Creating a Safe Space

My brain began to fill up with ideas about how I might help might white Christian brothers and sisters begin to understand the anger that was going on in Ferguson and in African American communities around the country. I thought to myself, "If white Christians do not understand the anger within the African American communities, then we can help them understand by providing a safe environment for them to ask their questions." I thought white and black Christians needed space to talk. We needed to create a space, a safe space, for them to come together. If we did this, many of our white Christian friends could get their questions answered. I thought, "If we do not provide a space like this, then where could white Christians in St. Louis go to have this type of discussion?"

I wrote up a proposal and submitted it to my pastor. The idea was that we would host a forum and I would invite several of my friends—African American pastors in the city—to sit on a panel. We would then allow our audience, primarily white Christians, to

48

ask questions anonymously via note cards. I also thought it would be necessary to have a few white Christians on the panel, so I invited a professor from Covenant Theological Seminary, and a local historian. Both men are committed to racial reconciliation and social justice. Since the death of Michael Brown had created a lot of questions, it made sense to me to invite my friend, Karen Thompson, who had been a teacher in the school district that Michael Brown attended. Karen taught Michael Brown when he was a sophomore in high school. We were creating space for this dialogue to happen between white and black Christians. But we were not sure if anyone would attend such a forum.

Once I got confirmation from all the speakers, it was time to promote the event. We invited several other predominantly white churches in the area. As we planned the event, we again wondered if anyone would show up. I was very concerned and my pastor was concerned as well. What if only ten people showed up? Or only thirty? Or only fifty? One way or the other we would get at least a small indication of the desire among white Christians to have open and honest dialogue about the issues around the death of Michael Brown and the Ferguson unrest.

We set the forum for a Saturday night in late November, which ironically was the day before the verdict on the shooting death of Michael Brown; however, we did not know that at the time. On that cold, rainy Saturday in November, we saw about two hundred people fill our sanctuary to dialogue about the death of Michael Brown and the events of Ferguson. The audience was mixed with whites and blacks, but the majority of the audience was white. As I looked at the audience, I thought to myself, "Scott was right. There are some white Christians who are interested in honest dialogue about what had gone on in Ferguson." We would go on to have an incredible night, and it would be the first of five forums we hosted around the city.

Race Conversations

If white and black Christians are going to close the emotional gap that exists between them, then space for dialogue has to be provided. Intentional time and effort must be created for conversation. From time to time, I ask my white Christian brothers and sisters if they grew up having conversation about race in their home and nine times out of ten the answer is, "No." On the other hand most of my black Christian brothers and sisters had conversations about race regularly from the time they were children. These conversations were not born out of the need for good, stimulating, dinner-time conversation; instead, they were born out of necessity because in certain situations, these conversations kept us safe. Whether in the car, in the yard, in the home, on the street, at church, they occurred whenever African American parents felt the need to have these conversations. They wanted to prepare their children for the reality of the world they were living in.

I remember one time when I was about eleven years old, a friend and I were going to walk to the store to buy either some candy or a toy. My mom stopped us and said, "If you do buy something, make sure you get a receipt. Always get a receipt!" Before I could ask my mom why, she said, "That way they cannot accuse you of stealing." This was an early introduction to the reality that there were some who might make assumptions about me based upon the color of my skin. On another occasion, my mom cautioned me about my behavior in public when out with my white friends. She told me I should not expect that those in authority (teachers, principals, policeman, etc.) would treat me the same as my white friends. She said, "You cannot do everything you see them do." These are just a few examples of the conversations many African American parents have with their kids.

As a result of these types of conversations, many African Americans become comfortable and proficient talking about racial matters. They are proficient in the sense that they have had these types of conversations from the time they were children. They have had time to process what these conversations reveal about themselves and the society in which they live, and can speak about the black experience in America.

Since many white Christians did not grow up talking about race, it is not an easy conversation to begin, and it can be very difficult. The idea of having a conversation about race with black Christians may cause extreme fear and anxiety for white Christians. I think many white Christians do not engage in conversations about race for a few reasons. First, there are varying degrees of ignorance about the life experiences of their black Christian brothers and sisters. For example, one day I went to lunch with one of my white Christian brothers who I had recently met at a racial reconciliation forum. The lunch was an intentional meeting we had set up to talk about our own personal experiences growing up in America. During our conversation, I asked my friend if there were many African Americans living in his neighborhood, or attending school with him. He responded, "Yes, but just a few." Without any further probing, he paused and said, "It never occurred to me until just now that their experience, as African Americans living in our neighborhood, could have been different from mine because they were African American." In this case, my white Christian friend was just ignorant about the experiences of his African American neighbors and classmates. To some degree, he might be limited in how well he could really engage in a conversation about race years ago because he did not know there might be some challenges with the experiences of blacks or black Christians in America.

Another reason why white Christians may not engage in conversations about race is because they are fearful that they may say something to offend their black Christian brother or sister. They do not want to be seen as racially insensitive or labeled as a racist. Their fear is understandable. I mean, who wants to be labeled a racist or racially insensitive? This fear alone is enough to keep white Christians from engaging in a conversation about race. Also, some white Christians may have had bad experiences, not necessarily with their black Christian brothers and sisters, but with other African Americans. This, too, can contribute to the fear.

A third reason white Christians might not engage in conversations about race is that they do not know what to do about it. They may have some knowledge of the issues and are even courageous enough to ask questions of their black Christian brothers and sisters, but at the end of the day, they do not know what they can personally do about it. This can leave white Christians feeling helpless and powerless about the race problems that exist within American society.

There are probably a myriad of other reasons white Christians do not engage in conversations about race, and we would need to ask them individually about their reasons. I however, want to mention one more reason: white Christians are a part of the dominant ethnic group in America. The dominant ethnic group within a society does not necessarily have the greatest number of people; they just need to have the greatest influence through authority, power, resources, and wealth. For example, during apartheid in South Africa from 1948-1994, white South Africans, who made up a minority of the population, held the power over the non-white South Africans. Those who are a part of the dominant group within a society are often ignorant of the experiences of the sub-dominant groups.

The Dominant Group

For most dominant groups, their cultural influence can create a perspective that limits the dominant group's ability to truly know what the experience is like for sub-dominant groups. However, the sub-dominant group's survival within the larger society depends on how much they know about the dominant culture and how well they can assimilate to it. The dominant group's survival does not depend on what they know about the sub-dominant group(s), whereas the survival of the subdominant group depends on their knowledge of the dominant group's language, norms, customs, history, and culture. White Christians are a part of the dominant group. This however does not make white Christians evil, bad, or oppressive, but it may make it harder for white Christians to identify where racial discrimination and inequality exists within American society. All ethnic groups have cultural norms; however, it can sometimes be difficult for the dominant culture to identify their own cultural norms because they set the cultural norms for the society. They may not see their norms as white cultural norms, but as simply societal norms.

For instance, if you ask someone who is white to identify a

white cultural norm, they may not be sure what exactly you are asking. They may not have ever realized that how they think and relate to time is a cultural norm. Have you ever heard this idea? If you are not five minutes early for a meeting, then you are late. This is a cultural norm that is not necessarily viewed the same way among black and Hispanic groups; however, both blacks and Hispanics understand this is an established norm within the broader American society. Both blacks and Hispanics view and approach time differently within their own ethnic circles. If you have spent a lot of time around blacks you may have heard the term "CPT" used. CPT stands for "colored people's time." CPT basically means that if you are hosting an event and inviting blacks to attend, for one reason or another, they will not show up until 20-30 minutes after the event begins. It is just part of our culture and how we relate to time and to one another. However, most of my black friends have assimilated into white culture and they understand how our white friends, bosses, and colleagues view time, so we have learned to make the adjustment. Time is just one of many cultural norms, and all ethnic groups have cultural norms.

Black Americans, Hispanic Americans, and white Americans, although they are all Americans, still have their own unique culture. They all have a unique history, food, language or dialect, customs, music, and values. But many whites are not aware that these things are culturally tied to white American culture, these things are just considered the norm for all Americans. This is why it may be hard for many white Americans and white Christians to understand the need for a BET (Black Entertainment Television) or Univision (American Spanish language broadcast television). The question from some white Americans is "Why do we need BET or Univision? And why do we need a Black Music Awards? And why do we need a Black History month?"

Most of these questions originate from a mindset that does not realize white Americans have a culture, and their culture is the dominant one. Right or wrong, this makes sense doesn't it? Any group that is in power will operate out of its own cultural norms and promote those norms among the broader society. For the sub-dominant groups in America, the culture of the dominant group is not necessarily their own. Certainly, there is overlap from the dominant culture to the sub-dominant cultures within a society, but the cultures are nevertheless different. So why is there a need for a BET, Univision, or Jet magazine? The simple answer is that Black, Hispanic, and other sub-dominant American groups have their own culture, which often is not promoted or considered by the dominant group.

The dominant group's experience within the society is usually very different than that of the sub-dominant group(s). Whereas the sub-dominant groups may easily see the lack of minority representation within the local or national government as a problem, it may have never occurred to those from the dominant group. As part of the dominant group in America, white Christians may share many of the same cultural blind spots as other white Americans. This blindness or unconscious bias towards their ethnic group and other ethnic groups (sub-dominant) can be a great obstacle to engaging in conversations about race, inequality, and justice. The encouraging thing is that these challenges can be overcome with education and openness.

Hard Work of Unity

If white and black Christian leaders can provide a regular, safe space for conversations about race in America and in the church, then we can begin to move past the emotional divide that exists between white and black Christians. On occasion, I will have a conversation with a white Christian friend who will tell me in one way or another that there is really no need for Christians to discuss racial issues. They will quote from Galatians 3:28: "There is neither Jew nor Greek, there is neither slave nor free, there is neither male nor female, for you are all one in Christ Jesus." I will agree with the declaration in that passage, and then I will quote Ephesians 5:31: "Therefore, a man shall leave his father and mother and hold fast to his wife, and the two shall become one flesh." I know that this passage is dealing with the joining of man and woman together sexually, but most people understand there is a practical side of marital oneness that has to be worked out. Anyone who

54

has been married for more than a week realizes that if there is going to be any unity between a husband and a wife, it will take intentional hard work (communication, understanding, apologies, and forgiveness, etc.). Generally, married Christian couples realize they are supposed to operate as a unified couple. And when I quote Ephesians 5:31, they often begin to see what I am getting at before I finish quoting the verse. They know marriage takes work and even though the Bible presents a husband and wife as one, the husband and wife must work to truly live as one.

The truth about true unity within the ethnically diverse body of Christ is that we have to do some hard, intentional work. Christ's redemption for us not only applies to our relationship with God but also to one another. However, since we are being sanctified (the ongoing work of the Spirit is making us more like Christ) but are not completely sanctified, we must work against all divisions in the body, whether ethnic, racial, or economic. In order to do this, we must be open and create space for intentional, personal, honest, welcoming dialogue about these issues.

Discussion Questions

1. Is it important for Christians and Christian leaders to create space for racial dialogue? Why/why not?

2. What makes discussions about race so difficult for white and black Christians?

3. What are some fears that potentially would keep you from engaging in dialogue about race with other Christians?

4. Do you agree many white Christians do not know what to say, to do, or what to think about racial issues? Explain your answer.

5. Do you believe unity in the body of Christ is something we need to work for, or is it a result of Christ's work on the cross?

6. What are some of the cultural issues that the ethnically diverse body of Christ might encounter now and in the future?

4

Certain Openness

"I find that when you open the door toward openness and transparency, a lot of people will follow you through."
—Kirsten Gillibrand

The week after Michael Brown's death, and in the first week of the Ferguson unrest, I felt anger, bitterness, and resentment growing inside of me, and I could not stop it. I kept praying, "Lord help me, Lord help me! Lord, help my heart. Lord, help my black son. Lord, help my black wife. Lord, help my black daughter! Lord, take the pain away. Lord, take the sadness away. Lord, take the fear away!"

This was a very confusing time for me because I love my white friends, colleagues, and members of my church, but it was hard to know if they saw the pain in the African American community over the death of Michael Brown. I was not primarily concerned with them analyzing the facts of the case as much as I wanted them to empathize and suffer along with me and other blacks. I wondered if my white Christian friends saw me as a black man, a black man like the black men they saw on television in Ferguson: the black men that were angry and protesting; the black men who had sons and were fearful their sons had no real protection under the law. I thought to myself, "What confidence can black parents have in the American legal system? How could anyone say to them, 'Your black son will be safe.'?"

I knew that my white colleagues and the white members in

our church loved me and my family, but I wondered if they saw us as a black family. Or did they unconsciously think, "Aaron and his family aren't black like those we see on TV." But those blacks they saw on TV during the Ferguson unrest were our people. They were black and middle to lower class. And although my family had moved into a working class white neighborhood in St. Louis, my family was a lower-middle working class black family and many of my relatives were lower class.

The church I grew up in was in Wellston, and my closest cousins lived in East St. Louis and Pine Lawn. Those places were where we spent a lot of our weekends. I was familiar with the frustrations of a people who seemed to have no voice. I was living simultaneously in the two different Americas that Dr. King wrote about in his speech, "The Other America." This was a speech Dr. King delivered at Gross Pointe High School outside Detroit, Michigan. The speech highlighted the socio-economic disparity between whites and blacks in America.

In the suburb where I lived, there were jobs, opportunity, resources, education, and ambition. In the city where my cousins lived, there were little resources, few jobs, dilapidated housing, failing schools, and extreme poverty. So I understood the protests in Ferguson were much deeper than the shooting death of Michael Brown. The protests were against something systemic: something systemic that seemed to disadvantage blacks. Many black Americans in Ferguson and around the country had little faith in the American legal system. The outrage was against the American legal system and its past rulings in favor of policemen who used lethal force toward blacks, particularly black men. This is not to say the police have never used appropriate and lethal force towards black men, but the numbers of these types of situations seem to highlight a deeper systemic and unconscious bias toward black males in America.

In Ta-Nehisi Coates' book, *Between the World and Me*, he argues that America, since its inception as a country, has had a long history of violence toward African Americans. I think many black Americans, from the time of slavery, the Jim Crow South, the Civil Rights movement of the 50's and 60's, the Watts riot in 1967,

L.A. riot in 1992, Ferguson riot of 2014, and to the Baltimore riot in 2015, would agree with Mr. Coates. At the heart of the protests in Ferguson and around the country was this question: How does American society view the lives of black Americans? This is really the question that gave rise to the BLM (Black Lives Matter) movement. I do not believe the BLM movement was ever saying that other American lives (White, Hispanic, Korean, etc.) or police lives do not matter; rather, it was a statement based on the historical and current violence toward blacks in America. The number of incidents of violence would suggest that black lives in America matter less than other ethnic groups, and in America all lives should matter equally.

Unconscious Bias

In a 2015 Washington Post article titled, "Aren't More White People than Black People Killed by Police? Yes, but No," journalist Wesley Lowry wrote:

> According to the most recent census data, there are nearly 160 million more white people in America than there are black people. White people make up roughly 62 percent of the U.S. population but only about 49 percent of those who are killed by police officers. African Americans, however, account for 24 percent of those fatally shot and killed by the police despite being just 13 percent of the U.S. population. As The Post noted in a new analysis published last week, that means black Americans are 2.5 times as likely as white Americans to be shot and killed by police officers. U.S. police officers have shot and killed the exact same number of unarmed white people as they have unarmed black people: 50 each. But because the white population is approximately five times larger than the black population, that means unarmed black Americans were five times as likely as unarmed white Americans to be shot and killed by a police officer.[1]

But what makes the question, "Aren't More White People than Black People Killed by Police?" hard to get at is that

[1] Lowery, Wesley, "Aren't More White People than Black Killed by Police? Yes, but No." *Washington Post*, July 11, 2016, accessed February 26, 2017.

59

much of what Americans may believe about the lives of black Americans are not primarily conscious but unconscious. We are all products of bias, particularly media bias. We are bombarded by images, sound bites, literature, books, magazines, TV shows, and movies that inform our thinking. Americans could consciously, in principle, value the lives of black Americans, but unconsciously see them as lazy, worthless, violent, uneducated, criminals, a threat, and a problem, which is arguably the major media narrative for black males in America. This is where the danger lies—in our unconscious bias. Do I believe in unconscious bias? Yes. Do I have unconscious bias? Yes. Am I aware of my unconscious bias? I try to be, but by virtue of it being unconscious, how could I be? What helps is when I acknowledge, in humility, my unconscious bias toward other groups, particularly ethnic groups. Then God reveals my unconscious bias, so that it becomes conscious bias, and now I can address it.

At this point, many people (and particularly many white Christians will push back against the notion of unconscious bias and say, "But you don't know my heart. I love everyone, and I do not discriminate against any other ethnic group. I have many African American friends." Consciously this may be true, but unconsciously it could be false. Often what reveals the unconscious bias we have towards others is how we feel on the inside when we see certain images which confirm our bias.

For example, many people believed the death of Michael Brown was justified because in their minds he was a thug, a thief, and a criminal; therefore, he deserved to die. That bias or unconscious bias for many did not allow them to see Michael Brown as a teenager preparing to start the next chapter of his life after graduating high school. They could not see him as a son of a mother who was very proud of him, or see him as a person who had his own fears, insecurities, and challenges as do most white teens his age in America. For many, this meta-narrative on Michael Brown is an extreme challenge to accept. On a side note, those who work in the media industry are very aware of the unconscious biases that prevail within a society. It is their business to know.

Charles Blow a writer for The New York Times wrote this in an op-ed titled, "Crime, Bias and Statistics":

What I find too often overlooked in this war of words is the intersection between the two positions, meaning the degree to which bias informs the statistics and vice versa.

The troubling association—in fact, over association —of blacks with criminality directly affects the way we think about both crime and blacks as a whole.

A damning report released by the Sentencing Project last week lays bare the bias and the interconnecting systemic structures that reinforce it and disproportionately affect African-Americans.

This is the kind of report that one really wants to publish in its totality, for its conclusion is such a powerful condemnation of the perversity of racial oppression. But alas, this being a newspaper column, that's not possible. Still, allow me to present many of their findings:

- "Whites are more punitive than blacks and Hispanics even though they experience less crime."
- "White Americans overestimate the proportion of crime committed by people of color and associate people of color with criminality. For example, white respondents in a 2010 survey overestimated the actual share of burglaries, illegal drug sales and juvenile crime committed by African-Americans by 20 percent to 30 percent."
- "White Americans who associate crime with blacks and Latinos are more likely to support punitive policies—including capital punishment and mandatory minimum sentencing—than whites with weaker racial associations of crime."[1]

In her book *Suspicion Nation*, Lisa Bloom says:

While whites can and do commit a great deal of minor and major crimes, the race as a whole is never tainted by those acts. But when blacks violate the law, all members of the race are considered suspect." Bloom adds, "The standard assumption that criminals are black and blacks are criminals is so prevalent that in one study, 60 percent of viewers who viewed a crime story with no picture of

[1] Blow, Charles M., "Crime, Bias, and Statistics." *The New York Times*, September 7, 2014, accessed February 26, 2017

the perpetrator falsely recalled seeing one, and of those, 70 percent believed he was African-American. When we think about crime, we 'see black,' even when it's not present at all.[1]

It seems that bias, including unconscious bias, is clearly a factor in the way Americans views African Americans. And I would think it is safe to say that many white evangelicals are under the influence of these same biases.

After the death of Michael Brown and the Ferguson riots, much of the unconscious bias from white Christians manifested itself on social media. The thoughts and comments in some cases revealed many years of unconscious bias toward African Americans, particularly African American males. Unfortunately, for some white Christians, the rioting, looting, and angry black faces confirmed the one consistent, prevailing media driven narrative about black Americans. Many quickly embraced the narrative without understanding the media's angle and asking good questions such as: Why is there so much anger being expressed by the African Americans in Ferguson and around the country? What has made them so angry? Am I missing part of this story? Do they have a right to be angry? Are there African Americans who are peacefully protesting? What I learned through a few racial reconciliation forums was that white Christians were asking some of these questions, and many were asking these questions for the first time in their lives.

A Surprising Openness

There was something about the reaction to the death of Michael Brown that captivated many white Americans and many white Christians. Many white Christians—and they were not alone—previously believed that as a nation we were further along in black and white race relations. How could we have a race riot in 2014? And how could we have protests about racial inequality around the country? It was like we had stepped back into the 1950's and

---

[1] Bloom, Lisa, *Suspicion Nation: The Inside Story of the Trayvon Martin Injustice and Why We Continue to Repeat It* (Berkley, CA: Counterpoint, 2014), cited in Blow, Charles M., "Crime, Bias, and Statistics," *New York Times*, September 7, 2014, accessed February 26, 2017

1960's at the height of the Civil Rights Movement. But it wasn't the 1950's. It was 2014, and here we were as a nation tackling this topic again. Many white Christians dared to ask themselves: Is there something that I am missing here? And could it be that African Americans have a different experience within American society even in 2014?

What I experienced in the many conversations I had with my white Christian brothers and sisters was an incredible openness and a willingness to engage in deep, meaningful conversations about race, racism, and inequality. This openness among white Christians was wide spread, at least in St. Louis and some other parts of Missouri. I often encountered members from predominantly white churches who informed me their church was hosting conversations and/or attending racial reconciliation conferences or reading books like *Divided by faith: Evangelical Religion and the Problem of Race in America* by Michael O. Emerson.

When we hosted the first forum, "Why So Much Anger?" at the Journey (West County) in November 2014, we had about 200 people show up. Of the people who attended, 85-90 percent were white Christians. When we held our second forum, "Racial Reconciliation in the Wake of Ferguson" in February 2015 (hosted by Pastor Michael Jones, an African American pastor whose church is located in the heart of North St. Louis), we bussed 90-100 white Christians from an affluent suburb in order to meet, eat together, and discuss racism in St. Louis and America. There were about 250 people who showed up, and the participants were almost split 50/50 black and white. It seemed clear to me that God was doing something new among white and black Christians.

This is not to say that forums, discussions, and even ministries about racial reconciliation had not occurred before 2014. Many of us were well acquainted with the work of John Perkins in the area of racial reconciliation among Christians. John Perkins is a true pioneer in this area as he began this type of work among evangelicals in the 70's. Perkins went on to found the John Perkins Center for Reconciliation, Leadership Training, and Community Development in 2004. So the Christian world is not necessarily new to the conversation of racial reconciliation and social justice; however, there is a new stirring, particularly among white evangelicals who live in white affluent areas of a city.

For years, many white Christians have been concerned about racial reconciliation and social justice issues. I think of churches like New City Fellowship, New City Fellowship South, and South City church in St. Louis. But these churches are located in the more urban or diverse areas of St. Louis. What I am encountering more and more is predominantly white Christian churches, located in affluent suburban neighborhoods, engaging in these conversations on a deeper level. And these are churches, in large part, who would acknowledge they generally have not had any sustainable dialogue or efforts toward racial reconciliation and social justice issues.

I believe that many white Americans and many white Christians assumed that we were further along as a country in the area of racial reconciliation between blacks and whites. We have made great strides as a country, but the unrest in Ferguson after the death of Michael Brown revealed there are still deep wounds within the African American community over racial inequality. It is this experience of racial inequality in America that blacks, and more specifically black Christians, can share with their white brothers and sisters to help provide a needed bridge to a better understanding of what that inequality looks like.

At the end of the first forum we encouraged the participants—mostly white and black Christians—to sit and talk for the remainder of the evening. We set up tables, coffee and snacks, and gave the participants 45 minutes to find someone of a different race to talk with. Most people stayed for 45 minutes to an hour. The following week at church, one of our white members came up to me and thanked me for hosting the forum. He told me that he was still processing some of the conversations he had that night with some of our black participants. He confessed that he was still having a hard time understanding the claim of inequality from the African Americans he spoke to that night, but he added their personal stories about inequality had a great impact on him. He then asked me if I had another story I could share with him, and I said, "Yes, I do."

In all of my diversity work before Ferguson, I had underestimated the power of a personal testimony to open the eyes of my white brothers and sisters. But the more conversations I had with my white brothers and sisters and the more forums we put on for white Christians, the more I heard testimonials from white Christians that it was the stories that really helped them begin to understand. Now, God has led white Christians all over the country to be open to the conversation of racial reconciliation and racial inequality in America. Black Christians must recognize this season and steward it well. We will need to be peaceful, patient, humble, and honest, speaking the truth in love. Now is the time to start the dialogue many white and black Christians have avoided for years. The dialogue is about racism and racial inequality in America and the church.

Discussion Questions

1. Do you think there is more racial dialogue occurring among white and black Christians since the death of Michael Brown?

2. In his book, *Between the World in Me*, Ta Nehisi Coates says that America has a long history of violence towards African Americans, particularly African American males. Do you agree with his assessment? Why or why not?

3. Do you think God has allowed the "conversation of race" to come to the church?

4. Why do you think white and black Christians have a different view of racism in America?

5. Are you open to having conversation with other Christians about race and racial injustice in America? Why or why not?

5

The Dialogue of Transformation

"Change happens by listening and then starting a dialogue with the people who are doing something you don't believe is right."
—Jane Goodall

The 1960's was a time when our nation was extremely racially divided. During that era, one of the most significant, ongoing, racial dialogues in American history took place between Dr. Martin Luther King Jr. and President Lyndon B. Johnson.

Dr. King was black and President Johnson was white. Both of these men grew up in the South: Dr. King was born in Atlanta, Georgia, and President Johnson was born in Stonewall, Texas. These men also grew up at a time and lived in a region of the country which allowed segregation between blacks and whites and enforced Jim Crow laws. Dr. King was a civil rights leader in the 50's and 60's, and Johnson was the Vice President under President John F. Kennedy from 1961-1963. He later became the 36th President when President Kennedy was assassinated in 1963.

Dr. King first met Lyndon B. Johnson while Johnson was serving as Vice President. It was then that the tracks of their relationship were laid. Early on in the relationship, it was clear these two men did not see eye to eye on every issue. In fact, the May 15, 1964 issue of Life magazine included an excerpt from King's book, *Why We Can't Wait*. The excerpt gave a little insight into the relationship between King and Johnson. Of Johnson, King wrote:

"I had been fortunate enough to meet Lyndon Johnson during his tenure as Vice President. He was not then a presidential aspirant and was searching for his role under a man who not only had a four-year term to complete but was confidently expected to serve out yet another term as Chief Executive. Therefore, the essential issues were easier to reach and were unclouded by political considerations. His approach to the problem of civil rights was not identical with mine—nor had I expected it to be. Yet his careful practicality was, nonetheless, clearly no mask to conceal indifference. His emotional and intellectual involvement was genuine and devoid of adornment. It was conspicuous that he was searching for a solution to a problem he knew to be a major shortcoming in American life."[1]

Although these two men had different perspectives on civil rights and racial inequality, they listened to one another, learned from one another, and worked with one another. Their on-going dialogue, helped to produce a civil rights bill that banned racial discrimination in public places, interstate commerce, the work place, and in housing. The trust they had with one another also allowed them to work together towards the Voting Rights Act, which banned discriminatory actions in Southern states that disenfranchised blacks from their right to vote. The ongoing dialogue between Dr. King and Lyndon B. Johnson changed each of them personally, and it brought great change to the country.

It Depends on the View

Once I realized why many of my white Christian friends and colleagues had not engaged in meaningful dialogue about the death of Michael Brown and the Ferguson unrest, I thought conversations between white and black Christians would be helpful. As I said earlier, I initially assumed my white colleagues and church members were not concerned about these issues, but I discovered there were good reasons why many of them had not engaged in this dialogue. Those who did engage were those who lived in an urban area or attended a multicultural or predominantly African

[1] King Jr., Martin Luther, *Why We Can't Wait* (London: First Signet Classic Printing, 1963), pp. 136-137.

American church. These white Christians seemed to be comfortable talking about issues of race, culture, systemic racism, and social justice issues. There seemed to be something about their regular contact and relationships with African Americans that granted them a different perspective on race matters. Also, those who lived in urban areas were able to see first-hand the inequality within the school system and hear stories from their African American friends and neighbors about their experiences with racial inequality. It seems this exposure to the African American community helps these Christians have a greater empathy and understanding of the racial divide in our country.

In *Divided by Faith*, Emerson and Smith acknowledge that whites living in ethnically and economically diverse neighborhoods tend to have a different view of racial inequality than whites who live in a predominantly white area of a city.[1] This makes sense doesn't it? A diverse neighborhood or church will have people who have different experiences and perspectives. When I say a diverse neighborhood, I do not necessarily mean a neighborhood that is extremely ethnically diverse but rather a neighborhood or church where the whites are in the minority. The church and/or neighborhood could be predominantly black and the whites who belong to either of those communities will probably have a different view on systemic racism and social justice issues. These whites will not only hear the experiences of their black neighbors or members, but they may witness the pain families experience in sending their children to an unaccredited failing public school. They will begin to view the world with a different cultural lens. However, this does not mean that every white person who lives in a diverse neighborhood will have eyes to see systemic racism, but I believe it is more likely.

Dialogue is the Key

Dialogue between white and black Christians in America is the key to a deeper unity within the body of Christ. For years, many white and black Christians have not ventured into a conversation

---

[1] Emerson and Smith, *Divided by Faith*, pp. 80-81.

about race with one another. As a teen, I had many white Christian friends with whom I went to church on a regular basis. I do not remember hearing any sermon, Bible study, or youth group message about racism or racial reconciliation between black and white Christians. Whenever I visited my white friends' churches, the people were always kind, loving, and accepting. I sometimes felt as if this, in a small way, was their method of racial reconciliation. I appreciated it very much. I felt the love of Christ, I really did, but I often wondered what they really thought about black people. I wondered what they thought about the blacks who were poor, uneducated, angry, and or frustrated with society—the type of blacks who had not grown up around white people and did not trust them. I wondered what they thought about the blacks who felt like the odds were stacked against them and those in power did not really care about them. What did they think about the blacks who were loud, proud, and often times confrontational? What would my white evangelical friends think about them? Did they see me as one of those kinds of black people?

In truth, they did not see me that way. I had learned to talk, as my cousins from East St. Louis and North City would say, "Like one of those white kids." I had learned to talk in a way that made it easier for me to fit in with my white friends. I think the technical term for it now is "code switching." I learned to talk one way around my cousins and another way around my white friends. For example, if I wanted one of my white friends to stop teasing me I might say, "Hey, Robbie, could you please stop calling me those names?" However, if I was on the eastside (East St. Louis) with my cousins, and they were teasing me I might say, "Hey, Lil Dudes! Yaw'll play too much. Just keep my name out yo mouth!" It did not take me too long to figure out that I needed to be able to code switch in order to operate in both worlds. It was clear to me that my white friends and my white Christian friends did not think of me as being black because I reminded them more of themselves than someone whom they would consider black. In fairness, they probably did not think much about it. They just saw me as Aaron.

I will take some responsibility for this because as a kid I

worked hard to fit in and I worked even harder not bring attention to my skin color. When I was in a group of white friends and I was the only black person in the group, I worked to stay away from topics, comments, or anything that might remind them I was black. I was afraid if they remembered I was black, then the black jokes would start, and I would have a decision to make—do I take the jokes or do I go home and be alone? Neither of those options was desirable for a young black boy who just wanted to play. So even though most of my white friends cared about me, they had no idea what thoughts went through my mind and neither did my white Christian friends. For them to really understand what it was like being an African American, we would need to have a long talk; we needed to have dialogue.

Dialogue Begins

I stood in front of 80 to 90 of my white church members, who had agreed to partner with a predominantly black church in North St. Louis City, to talk about racism and said,

> "This is the conversation that the church in America has needed to have for years, and that is the conversation about racism in America. Black and white churches have done unity services, joint worship services, service projects, and the like, but we have never sat down with one another and had the conversation about racism in America and more specifically racism in St. Louis. But tonight, we are going to have that conversation. And I believe we can do it; I believe we can have fruitful dialogue about racism. I know it can be a fearful thing to think about what might happen if we start this dialogue among black and white Christians, but I am reminded of a couple things that should humble all of us before we begin the dialogue. The first thing is that our individual sin levels the playing field among us and therefore we should not hold the racial biases, conscious or unconscious, against each other. We are all sinners in the hands of a merciful God who sent his son Jesus to die for us, and not one of us is perfect. We are all in the wonderful process of sanctification by which we are being made more and more like Christ. The second

thing is that Christ has redeemed us from our sin and although we need to confess those sins (1 John 1:9), Christ is willing to forgive us of any and all sins, even the sins of racism and bigotry. So if Christ is willing to forgive us of the sin of racism we should be willing to forgive one another. I am also confident that we can have this conversation because at the end of the day, this is a family conversation. We are family and we won't let this divide us (1 Cor. 12:25), because Christ has united us into one new man (Eph. 2:14-15). Thank you for being courageous!"

The idea of the forum was to bring our church—a predominantly white church located in an affluent, western suburb of St. Louis—together with a predominantly black church—in a northern urban area of St. Louis—in order to have conversations about race. We planned to have a meal together around tables and then have table discussions about racism. Before the evening began, we bussed in ninety church members from the suburbs, on a strategic route through the city to the church. We wanted our members to visually encounter the physical brokenness of inner-city St. Louis. My assumption was that many of our members had never been or had rarely spent time in North St. Louis City. Seeing dilapidated buildings tagged by graffiti, abandoned houses and businesses, vacant lots littered with glass, rocks and rubble, liquor stores, and low-income residents walking to their destinations, could all potentially help our members begin to understand systemic racism, generational poverty, and issues of inequality. We wanted our people to be confronted with a different reality than what they were used to. We wanted them to wrestle with their thoughts and emotions around the issue of race and hoped the bus ride would prime the pump.

When we arrived at Friendly Temple Missionary Baptist Church (FTMBC), a team of their staff came on the bus and greeted us. They boarded our busses and guided our bus drivers through the neighborhoods that surrounded their church. They wanted to show us the neighborhood and the people they served. They also wanted to show us how God had blessed them to serve the people in that community. One of their most impressive accomplishments was an apartment complex they constructed to provide low-income housing for people in need. Although the tour of the neighborhood and the facilities at FTMBC were not our idea, it also helped lay a great foundation for our later discussion on racism.

The evening began with prayer and a brief welcome and prayer from one of the ministers from FTMBC. Then a local historian gave a snapshot of St. Louis's racial history, which culminated with him speaking about the death of Michael Brown and the Ferguson Riots. This brought a silence to the mixed crowd of about two hundred and fifty people. To put both white and black participants at ease, I got up and reminded the group that we were family and that we needed each other. I then encouraged the group to take five minutes to go around the room and introduce themselves to people in the group that had a different "hue" of skin than their own. This seemed to put everyone at ease. Then we prepared to have dinner with one another.

Fruitful Dialogue

As both white and black participants made their way to the tables, I was fearful most people would sit with people they were comfortable with—those of their own skin color. In this case that would mean the black members would sit with their fellow black church members and the white members would do the same and sit with their fellow white church members. I was not about to let that happen. I had already told our members I was not going to waste their time. I told them, "We are going to have this conversation tonight." I was determined to get these white and black evangelical Christians around tables to share experiences and talk openly and honestly about racism. While both white and black members were still unsure about where to sit and with whom to sit, I said jokingly, "Hey if I see too many black people at one table I'm gonna split you up and if I see too many white people at one table I'm gonna split you up. I want this thing to look like pepper, a little white and a little black at every table." That comment made everyone laugh, put them at ease, and gave them some needed direction.

After my instructions, people made their way through the food line and then to their tables. At each table was a list of dinner questions, after dinner questions, and community norms. The dinner questions were basic, non-threatening, "getting to know each other" questions. We asked questions like, "Where did you grow up?" or "What was your childhood like?" or "What was your neighborhood like growing up?" Although these questions were easy conversation starters, they were strategic. Where and how a person grew up can lay an important foundation for a conversation about racism.

The after-dinner questions were a little more direct. We asked things like, "Do you think racism exists in America and/or St. Louis?" or "Do you know what systemic racism is? If so, do you think it exists?" or "Do you believe in inequality or do you believe that the same opportunity exists for all?" These questions were a little more challenging and had the potential for greater conflict. That is why we placed community norms at each table. Community norms are like rules of engagement for a discussion. We reviewed these earlier with the entire group but felt the need to put them on the tables and have one person read them to the group before they started the second set of questions.

After dinner, Pastor Scott Hickox took the mic and briefly talked about biblical racial reconciliation (Eph 2:11-22; 4:1-6; 1 Cor 12:25). Then he told the participants it was time to start the discussion. By this time, it seemed most of them were eager to start talking. As I walked around the room, I was in awe of the dialogue taking place. There they were, white and black Christians, sitting around tables, discussing racism in America and in St. Louis! But what was more important was the fact that both black and white participants were sharing their personal stories about racism. This is where the dialogue became invaluable. As many of the black evangelicals shared anecdote after anecdote of personal incidents highlighting individual and systemic racism, many of their white evangelical brothers and sisters began to see things in a way they had never noticed before.

One elderly, white gentleman came to me and said, "As a young man, I received countless jobs through the connections my dad had and it never occurred to me that this was not the reality for others. I sat across from a black gentleman this evening who told me of his struggles to get to college, get through college and find work, without any meaningful help from family or friends." This white gentleman, for a moment, had been invited into the world of the underprivileged. The dialogue provided an opportunity for this gentleman's paradigm to shift. There were also other whites who were aware of racism and systemic racism and shared their experiences with their black brothers and sisters. There were also black brothers and sisters, particularly the older ones, who talked optimistically about the progress in race relations they had seen in their lifetime. This was a good reminder, particularly for those who were feeling discouraged and disheartened about America and the church after the death of Michael Brown and the Ferguson Riots. This space is needed, and it is what black and white Christians will need to continue.

Intentional, focused, creative, regular dialogue is one of the keys to closing the emotional distance between white and black Christians. It is also one of the keys to conquering other deep divisions (ethnic, gender, tribal, etc.) within the body of Christ. Michael Emerson and his colleagues studied multicultural churches. One church, Wildcrest Baptist Church, served as an incubator, fostering a friendship between three men: one African American, one Hispanic, and one from the white Cajun culture of South Louisiana. "These men get together at one another's home, go to the movies together, pray together, support each other during times of stress, eat out together, and babysit each other's children."[1] Robert Jones had this to say about the men, "These experiences changed how congregants participated at church. Even more importantly, it generated considerable 'bridging capital' that changed congregants' perspectives on racial inequality issues and carried benefits into other institutions and into other areas of their lives."[2]

In Ephesians 4:1-6, Paul admonishes the church to continually work towards keeping "the unity of the Spirit." This is a re-

[1] Emerson and Smith. *Divided by Faith*, pp. 162-63.

[2] Jones, *The End of White Christian America*, p. 193.

minder we will always have to strive and work toward keeping unity within the body of Christ. We need to work toward a deeper unity, a stronger unity that is not fractured whenever a white police officer kills a black male or a black male kills a white police officer. If we are going to pursue unity in the midst of a racialized society, we must have regular, intentional dialogue and friendship between white and black Christians.

Discussion Questions

1. Why might some white Christians that live in urban areas have a different view of racial inequality than white Christians who live in a predominantly white neighborhood?

2. Why is dialogue between white and black Christians so important to racial reconciliation?

3. Describe the forum that was mentioned in the text. What did they do at the forum?

4. What are the potential benefits to hosting a forum like the one mentioned in the text?

5. Take a few minutes to brainstorm with your group about creating a forum that your church would host.

6

Regular Rythms

> "Unless you try to do something beyond what you have
> already mastered, you will never grow."
> —Ralph Waldo Emerson

When I was a freshman in high school, I took a class called keyboarding. It was really just a typing class. The class was full of freshman students just like me who had never learned to type before. I remember staring at the letters on the keyboard, confused by the fact the letters were not in alphabetical order. To me, it made better sense to set up the keyboard alphabetically, at least then you knew where to look for the letters.

Our teacher began by teaching us how to position our hands on the keyboard. It felt so awkward and unnatural to place my fingers in such a position. It was even more difficult to then type a word. Our teacher assured us that in time, we would get used to the positioning of our hands on the proper keys, and would also learn to strike the right keys without looking. I was doubtful, and by looking at some of the other students in the class, they felt the same way. How was she going to help us learn how to type this way?

After a few days of having us memorize the keyboard, the teacher told us we would do a typing drill. She handed us a piece of paper with a few simple words on them. The words went across the top of the page and had spaces in between them that separated the words into columns. We were instructed to type these same words across our paper. The teacher drilled us to see how many times we could type the list of words before the time expired. During the drill, we had to position our hands correctly on the keys and were not allowed to look at the keyboard while we were typing. After we did the drill the first time, our teacher notified us that every day at the beginning of class we would do our drill.

So every day, without exception, we did our typing drill. It became such a part of our daily class routine that students would enter the class talking to one another, pick up a drill sheet, sit down at a keyboard machine, insert a clean sheet of paper, and prepare for the drill, without ever ending their conversation. We definitely "knew the drill" so to speak. Those drills provided a necessary routine to help us learn how to type. It was our teacher who provided the necessary opportunity that helped transform us from students who could not type into students who could.

An Intentional Effort

I work at a private Christian school, and among my many roles, such as history teacher and coach, I also serve as the Director of Diversity. My role as Director of Diversity was initially created to foster sensitivity and awareness towards our students of color and their unique challenges as minorities in a predominantly white private school. Our school is a 7-12th grade private Christian school and is located in an affluent neighborhood. I am in my ninth year on staff, and over the years I have seen the number of students of color increase steadily. There are a little over a thousand students at the school, and our students of color make up a little more than 18 percent of the student body. African American students and international students from South Korea and China make up the largest percentage of our students of color.

Since I arrived at the school in 2008, God has sovereignly allowed our student body to become more and more diverse. At the beginning of the 2015-16 school year, we had over one hundred African American students and close to thirty international students. Although God has been faithful to bring families of color to our school, he has also used people like our former Head of

School to nurture a heart and vision for a diverse student body and community.

Our former Head of School was at the school for over twenty-five years and having a diverse study body was very important to him. In fact, he was the one who hired me because he believed our school needed to increase the diversity of its faculty. When I arrived at the school in 2008, there was one full-time African American teacher and two full-time African American staff. One was an office manager and the other was a custodian. But the Head of School had a vision for the school. In the spring of 2009, during a conversation about diversity and the school's future, I asked him this question, "Why does Westminster, or why do you, want to pursue diversity?" He answered, "I believe our school should reflect the diversity of the Kingdom of God. In the Kingdom of God there is ethnic diversity, socio-economic diversity, and diversity in church affiliation." That was good enough for me; I was sold. From that point on, I was willing to help our Head of School in whatever way I could to see our school become a more diverse community. This was not my vision; it was the vision from the Head of School. He would say it wasn't only his vision, but God's vision for our school as well.

In 2008 the students of color at our school made up about 14 percent of our student body, but by 2016, that percentage had increased to a little over 18 percent. I believe this was due to the vision and the intentional effort of not only the Head of School and others in the administration, but also on the part of our admissions director, who was and still is relentless in reaching out to minority families. Before I even began working at the school, the Head of School and the admissions director, both thought that a diverse student body should be a priority. In fact, the school already had a Diversity Committee made up of teachers, students, parents, and administrators. The committee was formed to help the school become a more diverse community. The Head of School was the chairman of the committee—which says a lot. The Head of School ran the committee, but the admissions director was also a part of the meeting and she took the minutes.

The more I talked with the Head of School and the Admissions Director, the more I realized their heart for a diverse community had deep roots. Years before I arrived at the school, the Admissions Director regularly attended network meetings for Diversity Directors in local Private schools. Although at the time our school did not have a Diversity Director, our Admissions Director felt the need to attend these meetings. She wanted to keep up with what was going on in the world of diversity in independent schools. Once I arrived and expressed an interest in helping our school in the area of diversity I soon began to attend these meeting with her and eventually I started to attend them by myself.

As I regularly attended these meetings, I was not only introduced to the world of private, independent, elite schools, but to their diversity programs as well. I also became aware of trainings, conferences, and workshops, that helped prepare Diversity Directors within independent schools. Although most of these schools did not embrace a biblical view of diversity, I was able to see the value and benefit of some of the things they shared with me. It was a short time after this I walked into the Head of School's office and told him I desired to be trained as a diversity director. I also added that I wanted the best training in the country. After seeing my zeal for this new role, the Head of School provided ongoing opportunities for training as a diversity director. It was clear to both me and the Head of School, that this role was the reason God had brought me here. We also knew that what God desired in this role for me at this Christian school would look very different from what it would look like in other private, independent institutions.

In 2009, I unofficially began working as the director of diversity, and in 2011 my position was official: I was commissioned by the Head of School and the Board of Directors to help the school become a diverse community. As a diversity director, one of my main responsibilities was to create cultural sensitivity and awareness among our student body and community. We wanted our minority student population to grow, thrive, connect, and feel a part of our school community.

I knew at the outset if I was going to help our school to become a more culturally sensitive community, I had to educate students and staff. I have spent most of my life straddling two worlds, the black world and the white world. And having lived in both worlds—the black world and the white world—I understood there is often a lot of misconceptions and ignorance which leads to misunderstanding. I knew enough about ethnic cultures to understand that each culture has a set of norms. And if these norms are not known or understood by both groups, it could be grossly offensive.

For example, in my second year at the school I decided to grow an Afro. In my first year at the school I wore my hair short, very close to my head, but then I decided to grow my hair out. My white students, and even some of my colleagues, were fascinated with my Afro. It was spongy with very tight small curls you could only see if you were very close to me. My hair was raised and stood-up away from my scalp. It was a smaller version of the Afro Michael Jackson wore as a kid, when he was a part of the famous Motown group, The Jackson Five. My hair was very different from any of my white students' hair, which made for some very interesting conversations about hair. The conversations also gave me an opportunity to educate students about other aspects of African American culture. There were a few students that were extremely fascinated by my hair. I could tell they wanted to touch it. One day, as we were leaving the classroom, one of the white male students standing behind me patted me on the head. It caught me by surprise. When I turned around to address him, he looked terrified and apologized. I smiled and said, "It is ok you want to touch my hair. I know it is very different from yours. Just ask me first." I added, "In the future you probably should not just assume you can touch a black person's hair. It can be interpreted as being disrespectful and demeaning. It can also cause a black person to feel violated." I explained to him he had violated my personal space by touching my hair without asking. To his credit, he listened to every word I said. He responded by saying he had not thought about it like that, but that he could see now that he had indeed violated my personal space. Through our discussion, I taught my student there are cultural norms in the African American community. I saw one of my primary tasks as director of diversity was to educate the community on issues of diversity, race, and culture.

Rhythms of Change

One of the first lessons I learned in my diversity director training was that the work of diversity is never done. This means the work of diversity within an institution is about changing a culture, and cultures do not change quickly. This is true of any institution, whether it is a school, a company, an organization, or a church. As our Head of School said to me early on, "Aaron, it takes a long time to change a culture, but I believe it can change." He said this because he did not want me to be discouraged by slow progress. I understood that the work of diversity was ongoing work—slow, hard work—but profitable work. As an educator, this freed my mind to take time and think about what regular rhythms I could create for teachers, faculty, staff, students, and parents that would help them grow in their cultural understanding. Rhythms are steps you take regularly that help to change a culture.

For example, written into our school's 3-5 year strategic plan is an initiative that requires the staff to receive some sort of diversity awareness training two times a year. A few years ago, I trained our staff on the topic of microaggressions. Microaggressions are subtle actions and/or words that may contain unconscious hostility toward someone of another race, gender, or any other group. An example of a microaggression would be me telling a woman, "You are pretty strong for a woman." What is being implied here? It implies that women are weak and this particular woman is an exception to the rule. In her book *Why Are All of the Black Kids Sitting Together in the Cafeteria?* author and professor Beverly Daniel Tatum records a conversation she overheard between two of her white students: "Yeah, I just found out that Cleopatra was actually a Black woman." "What?" the second student exclaimed in disbelief and then added, "That can't be true Cleopatra was beautiful."[1] This type of comment may be classified as a macroaggression. What was implied in the second student's response? It implied

---

[1] Tatum, *Why are All the Black Kids Sitting Together in the Cafeteria?*, p. 5.

that black women are not beautiful. My training on microaggressions was just one of many rhythms I tried to initiate over the years at the school.

Another rhythm was lunch conversations between students of color and teachers. I selected 6-10 students to sit down and eat lunch with teachers who had signed up. I facilitated discussion through questions. The idea was to give students of color an opportunity to share with the teachers about what it is like being a student of color at our school. The teachers were also able to ask the students specific questions. This allowed the students of color to be heard and validated. It also gave the teachers valuable information that helped them address the unique challenges and needs of the students of color.

Other rhythms included suggested books and articles for the faculty, as well as videos and movies I thought were conducive to cultural awareness. School-wide events like a Black History Month program and an International Week are also rhythms we used to help create an environment that is more aware and sensitive to other cultures.

Rhythms arc key to any institution that is trying to educate and transform its culture. But rhythms have to be intentional, strategic, and routine. Communities should have monthly rhythms, such as a newsletter. Other rhythms should occur quarterly, like a book study or a workshop. And still other rhythms, like trainings and events, should occur 1-2 times a year. These rhythms help people to grow in their understanding. If an institution has a strategic plan, and they desire change in the area of diversity or cultural awareness, they should include initiatives in their plan that help them achieve their goals. But if the institution or organization does not have a strategic plan or a document outlining goals and initiatives, it is unlikely they will ever see sustainable change. Rhythms help bring change.

Beginning Rhythms

As we think about racial dialogue between white and black Christians, we must understand that one conversation, one unity service, or one city project is not enough to make us comfortable talking about race or to change our thinking. If there is going to be helpful, beautiful transformation in our thinking, we will need many conversations; we will need regular rhythms. This is unchartered waters for many Christian churches in America. Most churches do not regularly address issues of race. I think many white Christian churches would agree that there are still race issues in America; however, they do not know how to address them as a church.

For this reason I founded an organization called Relate2Color in 2014. Relate2Color is an agency that works primarily with churches and para-church organizations on issues of race and culture. Relate2Color provides consulting, trainings, workshops, keynote speakers, strategic planning, and community forums. I founded Relate2Color because as Diversity Director, I recognized most American institutions (companies, businesses, colleges, etc.) either have diversity practitioners working for them, or they work with diversity firms. But for churches and Christian organizations, no such firms existed. There was and still is a need for churches and Christian organizations to have help dealing with issues of race and culture.

One of the things I suggest to a church that desires to address the issue of racism is to start a rhythm. Before I suggest anything to a church, I always ask the pastor and/or leadership: "What is the problem for which you need my help to solve?" Often, the problem centers on starting a dialogue about race. Other times it may deal with members who are ignorant and limited in their interactions with blacks. And other times it is something more specific, like addressing an event like the Ferguson riots or a topic like "Privilege." Whatever I recommend to the church, I prescribe it as a rhythm, something that is ongoing and will continue to help the church. I may prescribe an annual racial reconciliation dinner and discussion between a predominantly white and predominantly black church. I might also suggest the church leadership (pastors, elders, deacons, staff, etc.) do a book study twice a year with a focused discussion, and even encourage the congregation to read the book and discuss it together as a church.

My point is that if a church wants to help their congregation address racism in a lasting and effective way, they must establish rhythms. The rhythms can vary from year to year but the key is to have regular, creative opportunities for a congregation to grow. Every church should see these rhythms as regular maintenance and repair for racial unity within the body of Christ.

All successful businesses and companies have rhythms that help them understand who they are and who they need to become. Regular trainings, meetings, professional development, newsletters, speakers, books, articles, and the like are all rhythms that unify a business or company. If the Christian church is going to have an answer and a response to racism in America, we will need to be intentional with rhythms that help congregations grow and become skilled in racial conversations. These efforts will eventually lead to transformation and a deeper unity in the ethnically diverse body of Christ.

Discussion Questions

1. What are rhythms?

2. Who should establish rhythms for a church?

3. Why did the Head of School mentioned in this chapter want to pursue diversity?

4. How might a strategic plan help a church in the area of diversity or diversity related issues?

5. What were some of the rhythms established at the school mentioned in this chapter?

6. What might be some rhythms that a church (your church) might establish?

7

The Leader's Response

"There are times when a leader must move out ahead
of the flock, go off in a new direction, confident that he
is leading his people the right way."
—Nelson Mandela

In 2003 I took a job at an alternative school in St. Louis. This alternative school was not a tech school, but it was a school designed for students who were serving long-term suspensions. These students were serving either a 90 or 180 day suspension for extreme school violations. The school was designed to give students who were serving a long-term suspension an opportunity to continue their education until they were reinstated.

It was a challenging place to work, but I loved the students. The principal of the school was a warm and peaceful man with a great sense of humor. He had the perfect temperament to deal with students who could be very angry and explosive. I later discovered he was a Christian, which accelerated our friendship and admiration for one another. We were kindred spirits and both felt the students needed a lot of love, prayer, understanding and a little correction. Both of us felt a heavy burden for the students. Many of them were "street kids" from low-income neighborhoods where drugs and gang activity were not uncommon.

After several months on the job, my burden for the students grew overwhelming. In addition, there was a growing friction between some of the students and the teachers. A few of the teachers felt the students just needed more and harsher discipline. Some became very punitive in response to the student's behavior.

I prayed about the situation for a few days and decided I needed to start a faculty prayer group at the school. I knew this could be risky because not all the teachers and staff were believers, and it was a public school. I also did not know how our building principal would react to the idea. Would asking him to start a prayer group put him in an awkward spot with our non-believing teachers and staff? Would he be fearful that his superiors would reprimand him for it? I decided to ask him.

He did not respond immediately; he just sat in his chair with his hand under his chin, and his eyes staring down at his desk. I could tell he was considering what this might communicate to the teachers, the staff, the students, and his boss. An eternity seemed to pass as we sat in silence. I grew nervous and anxious. Had I put him in an uncomfortable spot? Was he angry with me now? Was this too much too soon?

I began to regret asking him, but then he broke the silence. "Mr. Layton, that is a great idea. Our kids do need a lot of prayer and it would be good to have a regular time to pray for them." He then asked me some specifics about the faculty prayer, which I was pleased to answer. As I answered his questions, he shared with me that he did not believe he should be the one to lead the faculty prayer. He did not want faculty members to think he would be upset with them for not attending. He would give his full support and provide whatever I needed to make the faculty prayer successful. He even offered his office as a meeting place for the prayer time.

So we began a weekly faculty prayer meeting. We met in the principal's office after school, and he was always present. On the days we had faculty prayer, our principal would come by my office a few minutes before school was out and say, "Remember we have faculty prayer this afternoon." I am not sure if he believed I would actually forget; I think it was his way of telling me the faculty prayer was important to him. He also regularly expressed to me that he wanted us to keep the faculty prayer going.

We eventually saw a few more faculty members join us. The prayer time eventually became an essential part of our school routine. Although the faculty prayer was my idea, it would not have happened without the support of the principal. He did not have to be the one who led the prayer, but he needed to support it, promote it, and show up. Other faculty members saw his support and began to support it as well. The support of the principal was key to the success of the prayer meeting.

An Example of Leadership

When I arrived at the private Christian school in the fall of 2008, I had no idea what was going on or what had been going on in the heart and mind of the Head of School. It turns out he was originally from New Jersey, and had grown up in a diverse neighborhood as a child. He had grown up with an appreciation for diversity, so when he became the Head of School in the mid-eighties, he arrived with an appreciation for a diverse community. Upon arriving in St. Louis, he and his wife sought out a church with a diverse congregation. The church had a mid-city location—it was situated at a nexus between the city and the suburbs—and was a truly multi-cultural church. He and his family are still members of that church today.

For many years, the school's student body and faculty had remained predominantly white. However it was the constant desire of the Head of School to have a school that would in some way reflect the diversity described in Revelation 7:9: "After this I looked, and behold, a great multitude that no one could number, from every nation, from all tribes and peoples and languages, standing before the throne and before the Lamb, clothed in white robes, with palm branches in their hands." But this dream would prove to be a challenge because the school was located in a predominantly white affluent suburb, which lacked ethnic diversity. However, because of the school's excellent reputation as a premier private Christian school, it would attract a few families of color through the 80's, 90's and early 2000's. Although the school did not initially attract a lot of minorities, a few more African American students began to enroll in the late nineties. This increased the number of students of color at the school. However, by the early 2000's, students of color still only made up less than 1 percent of the school's student body. Many of the African American students who had enrolled at the school later acknowledged it was a major adjustment for them. There were social issues for the students, like being the only black student in a class of white students, and having to discuss slavery, and civil rights, or books like *To Kill A Mockingbird*, in a classroom of white students and a white teacher. There were also cultural challenges that stemmed from stereotypes, assumptions, and biases about African American students, from some of their white classmates. These challenges, however, are not uncommon for minority students entering private, elite schools.

At some point, these concerns came to the Head of School and he wanted to put some things in place that would help African American students transition better and feel part of the school community. He then formed a committee made up of parents, teachers students, and administrators, and later called it the Diversity Committee. In reality, the Diversity Committee was more like a focus group which met regularly to voice and discuss concerns about issues of diversity at the school.

After hearing the Diversity Committee's concerns, the Head of School decided to address his administrative team. In a meeting, he asked them questions like: Who are we as a school? Who do we serve? Who are considered covenant children? All these questions led the Head of School and the administrative team to realize that if the school was going to grow in its diversity, they would need to be intentional. The Head of School, along with a strategic planning committee, wrote into the strategic plan initiatives designed to retain and increase the number of students of color at the school. There were also initiatives designed to increase the number of faculty members of color. The Head of School knew that if the school's desire to grow in diversity was not tied to their strategic plan, not much would change. The strategic plan would hold the Head of School, the administrative team, the teachers, and the faculty accountable to action and would also remind them of their specific commitment to diversity. I learned later that my being hired was a result of this strategic plan. It is now 2017, some nine years after that original strategic plan was implemented, and the students of color at our school make up over 18 percent of the student body.

I was hired in the hope that I would help the school increase its diversity. In the spring of 2009, I piloted the school's first diversity program. Eight years later, the diversity initiatives continue to move forward. Even though I coordinated and directed the programs, the former Head of School, who retired in 2012, supported and promoted these programs. As the leader of our school, he had the authority to give opportunities to address the faculty, provide trainings, and promote ideas. I may have been doing the work, but without the leader—without the Head of School supporting my ideas—the diversity program at our school would never have flourished. Our Head of School knew the importance of his support. I may have brought the zeal, desire, and passion, but because he was the leader, he was the key to it all.

The Pastor is Key

If white and black Christian churches are going to move forward in addressing issues of racism, they will need to have pastors and/or leaders who promote and provide opportunities for the congregation to grow in diversity. The pastor is the key. If the pastor supports and promotes conversations on racism, those conversations will move forward. If the pastor does not support them, they will fizzle out. The pastor can be the one who is leading the charge, but he does not have to be the one actually doing all the work. He can delegate the task to someone he feels is more capable, more passionate, or who has more time to dedicate.

For example, after the Ferguson unrest, my pastor asked me to lead our church in pursuing racial reconciliation. I then set up opportunities for our church to have ongoing dialogues about racism. One night, I organized a panel discussion with African American pastors from the inner-city. On another night, we set up a dinner and a round table discussion with an African American church in the city. I also set up a movie night where we invited three churches to come together, watch the movie Selma, and then have small group discussions afterwards. Through all of these events, I had my pastor's full support, which made all the difference. The pastor also supported me from the pulpit; he listed the events in the bulletin and announced them from the pulpit. He let the people know this was important to God and important to him. My pastor attended and took part in almost all of these events. I cannot stress enough just how important a pastor's support is in helping his congregation grow in this area.

In some cases, a pastor may want to put together some sort of task force or group to provide ongoing opportunities for growth. I have done some work with a few churches who have established a task force to assist the church in pursuing racial reconciliation and social justice issues. These churches have a group of people who have a heart for racial reconciliation, and are working against inequality and injustice. One of these groups met together long before they called me in as a consultant. Their team has succeeded in keeping the dialogue about racism and inequality alive at their church. They also set up multiple meetings with an African American church in the same community. Groups like these are a great way to provide ongoing opportunities for a church.

My home church put together a diversity task force. This group was tasked with looking at our church's overall diversity, how we might grow in diversity, as well as how to create conversations around issues of race and culture. Unless there is a person on group responsible for a church's racial reconciliation efforts, the church will find itself in the same spot 3-5 years later, without any major transformation in the congregation's thinking. Every church that wants to change can change. I have seen the results in certain churches in our city, because their pastors and their leadership are committed to racial reconciliation. They schedule regular meetings for their congregation and host yearly conferences. Churches can be committed to racial reconciliation, but such reconciliation won't happen without the support of the pastor and other church leaders being willing to own the responsibility of providing opportunities for the congregation.

Challenges Ahead

Now that I have stressed the importance of the leaders' support, I now want to help pastors and leaders understand the challenges involved in this type of work, particularly as it relates to key church leaders and the congregation. Pastors and leaders must realize that not every church leader, staff member, elder, deacon, or church member will agree with an initiative to address racial reconciliation. Pastors and leaders need to be prepared for some degree of pushback. This is especially true with regards to the congregation; some members will push back openly, while others will push back in private conversations with members or staff. You may hear comments such as: "Why are we always talking about race now? Talking about racism just makes things worse! Our church is losing its focus! We need to be focused on the gospel! I am tired of hearing about racism!" Others may just simply leave. It would be great if everyone was supportive, but most likely that will not be the case, and that is okay.

People have fears about discussing race, and church leaders, staff, and members are no exception. But if the pastor and church leaders are prepared to answer questions and give solid, biblical reasons for pursuing racial reconciliation, then many people in the church will be willing to give the pastor the benefit of the doubt. The pastor and/or church leaders must be patient and not try to move the congregation too fast. As I mentioned earlier, paradigms take time to change. If leaders are providing opportunities for dialogue 2-4 times a year, that is probably a good pace. If there are some members who would like to move a little faster, leaders can encourage them to do a few book studies over the course of a year and invite other members to join them. Or maybe they could do an optional 5-week racial reconciliation class or bible study. The reality is that you will have some members who will need to go slow, and others who desire to move a little faster, and others who do not want to move forward at all.

Helpful Hints

The Work is Biblical

As the pastor and/or leaders are moving their members along, here are some helpful things to share with the congregation. First, a church's commitment to racial reconciliation is biblical. Ephesians 4:1-6 captures the idea that believers should be ever striving to keep the peace with each other. The tone of this passage implies this is an ongoing and intentional work towards peace and unity. The body of Christ is ethnically diverse, and whatever racial, ethnic, and cultural divisions exist, we must work against them. Regular, intentional dialogue is necessary if white and black Christians are going to work through racial issues towards a deeper, stronger unity—a unity that is not easily fractured when there are reports of major racial issues on TV or social media.

A church's commitment to racial reconciliation is a powerful message from white Christians to their black Christian brothers and sisters that says, "I want to hear and understand your pain so that I may enter into it with you." 1 Corinthians 12:25-26 says, "…that there may be no division in the body, but that the members may have the same care for one another. If one member suffers, all suffer together." Every ethnic group has issues, but there are a unique set of problems African Americans have faced since the founding of this country. Though today, the problems are different in many ways, we still face racial difficulties. Black Christians are asking white Christian brothers and sisters to listen, hear, understand, enter into that suffering, and work with us for change.

Justice is Biblical

The second thing a pastor could say to his congregation about committing to racial reconciliation is that intentional effort will help transform our minds regarding poor, needy, and oppressed African Americans. It is not the middle to upper-middle class blacks that white Christians have problems with; it is generally the poor, uneducated blacks. Racial reconciliation opportunities between white and black Christians allow white Christians to understand that middle to upper-middle class black Christians often have some of the same feelings as poor blacks do. They also feel powerless in a society where the power structure tends to be led by whites.

For example, although many of my black friends did not take part in the rioting that occurred in Ferguson, we shared the anger of those who rioted. As we watched the rioting—which none of us condoned—we understood the pain, anger, and hopelessness. If black Christians had an opportunity to share some of these experiences with their white Christian brothers and sisters, it would not only help white Christians understand what middle class blacks feel, it could also help them empathize with poor blacks. This could lay a proper foundation for a church's outreach to poor and needy blacks.

As far as social justice goes, the Bible is replete with passages which reveal that biblical justice, the acknowledgment of it, the practice of it, and the defense of it, is what all God's people are called to do. In the book of Micah, the prophet announced the coming judgment on Israel and Judah because of their unfaithfulness to him. In chapter six, the prophet revealed exactly what God desires from them. The people assumed God required more sacrifices and more offerings. "With what shall I come before the Lord, and bow myself before God on high? Shall I come . . . with burnt offerings . . . with thousands of rams . . . with ten thousands of rivers of oil? Shall I give my firstborn for my transgression, the fruit of my body for the sin of my soul?" (Mic. 6:6-7).

It is as if the prophet expressed the heart of the people. It seemed to be a sincere and honest inquiry. But in verse 8, Micah revealed what God really desires, "He has told you, O man, what is good; and what does the Lord require of you but to do justice, and to love kindness, and to walk humbly with your God?"

It is fascinating to me that the Lord emphasized doing justice as the greatest requirement of their repentance. It is not that the Israelite's sacrifices and offerings held no value, but "doing justice," and the attitude of "loving kindness" were the priority. These were probably the practices that were most neglected. I think this passage reveals an aspect of the heart of God that many Christians overlook. Doing and defending justice—to and for others—are of the utmost importance to God.

In his book, *Generous Justice*, Tim Keller says that the Hebrew word for justice in Micah 6:8 is the word *mishpat*. In explaining the term Keller says this,

> Its most basic meaning is to treat people equitably. So Leviticus 24:22 warns Israel to "have the same mishpat ['rule of law'] for foreigner as the native." Mishpat means acquitting or punishing every person on the merits of the case regardless of race or social status. Anyone who does the same wrong should be given the same penalty. But mishpat also means to give people their rights. Deuteronomy 18 directs that the priests of the tabernacle should be supported by a certain percentage of the people's income. This support is described as "the priests' mishpat," which means their due or their right. So we read, "Defend the rights of the poor and needy" (Proverbs 31:9). Mishpat, then is giving people what they are due, whether punishment or protection or care.[1]

As people of God, it is our responsibility to "do justice" out of a heart of "mercy," particularly for those who are the most vulnerable within our society: those who need their rights defended and the ones who need advocates. In the Bible, there are passages that mention several classes of persons, often called "the quartet of the vulnerable."[2] They are the widows, orphans, immigrants, and the poor. Many times in the Old Testament when you see the word *mishpat*, you see these classes of persons.[3] "This is what the LORD Almighty says: Administer true justice; show mercy and compassion to one another. Do not oppress the widow or the fatherless, the immigrant or the poor" (Zech. 7:9-10).

We are called as the people of God to take up the cause to defend the rights of the widows, orphans, immigrants, and the poor. But we should also be mindful of other classes of persons (elderly, un-educated, disabled, foreigners, ex-convicts, etc.), who are not listed among these four classes who might also be in need.

---

[1] Keller, Timothy, *Generous Justice: How God's Grace Makes Us Just* (New York: Riverhead Books, 2012), pp. 3-4.

[2] Wolterstorff, Nicholas, *Justice: Rights and Wrongs* (Princeton University Press, 2008), p. 75.

[3] Keller, *Generous Justice,* p. 4.

Our task as the people of God is to care for all who are vulnerable within our society. We must be a voice for those who are voiceless. We must defend their rights (Prov. 31:8-9).

I believe every church can and should be committed to ongoing racial reconciliation, because at the end of the day it is an issue of unity in the body of Christ. I also believe that every church should actively pursue social justice within their communities, because it is who Jesus was (Isa. 1:17; 58:6-7), and it is who we are called to be.

In any organization, company, or institution, the person in charge is the person who will ultimately be responsible for any initiative that moves forward. It is also the case in a church that desires commitment to racial reconciliation: the pastor is the key. Although the pastor does not have to be the person actually moving the initiative forward, he has to actively support it and challenge and convince his congregation to participate. The pastor of a predominantly white church must understand that some of his leaders and members may not agree with this direction; however, his congregation will never grow to understand their black Christian brothers and sisters without regular opportunities that he, or someone he appoints, provides. Pastors must recognize they can help solve the problem of racial division in their city and in America, but it must begin with their church. The church must take action.

Discussion Questions

1. Why are pastors and church leaders key in a church's ongoing pursuit of racial reconciliation?

2. Can you think of some Scripture references that encourage the church to be committed to racial reconciliation?

3. What is the benefit of pastors and church leaders providing opportunities for their congregations to grow in their understanding of racial issues?

4. Why might it be a good idea for a pastor to put together a task force to provide ongoing opportunities for the congregation to grow?

5. What are some of the challenges a pastor may face if he decides to commit the church to the ongoing work of racial reconciliation?

6. How can pastors prepare their congregations for the ongoing work of racial reconciliation?

8

What Is at Stake

"Yesterday is not ours to recover, but tomorrow
is ours to win or lose."
—Lyndon B. Johnson

When I was in college, I played on the college baseball team. It was made up of players from several different states. We even had a player who was an international student from Japan. Some of the players were from rural areas, some were from the suburbs, and some were from urban areas. For the most part, none of us had ever met or even seen one another before becoming part of the team. We were all very different, but we had been selected by the baseball coach to come and play for the school.

The first few weeks of practice were a little awkward because we were strangers to one another. We spent several hours each day training, conditioning, hitting, throwing, and fielding. We also had regular team meetings. After a while, we grew more comfortable with each other and attending practice was no longer awkward. However, it still did not feel like we were a team, it just felt like we were a group of guys who had common passion and skill for the game of baseball.

As we neared our first game, the coach called a team meeting and spoke to us, calling us to team unity. "You are brothers and we are family and we play for each other. You play for the man next to you and he will play for you. Our common goal is to compete, as hard as we can and to win!" After that message, I finally felt like we were a team. As the season went on, we went through highs and lows as most teams do: we won some games and lost some games. But with each game, practice, and road trip, it felt more and more like we were a team and more and more like we were a family.

In my first year on the team, there were only two black players, and although many of our white teammates had come from communities where there were not a lot of blacks, we still felt like part of the team. We all believed our coach's message. One day, I was in the on-deck circle waiting to take batting practice and overheard two of my white teammates talking about interracial dating. It appeared that one of the black basketball players began dating an attractive white female volleyball player. The volleyball player was well known and well-liked by both male and female athletes at the school. She was a nice girl and had not dated anyone, so it was a surprise to learn that she would date a black basketball player from Memphis. "That's a nice looking girl!" said one of them, "Yes, she is a pretty girl. I just don't get it. It just ain't right either. It just ain't right for them to be together. I don't believe in that. I told my girlfriend that even if we broke up, I better never catch her dating a black guy!"

I had already moved closer to my teammates, hoping that my presence would deter the conversation, but without acknowledging my presence, they continued the conversation. I was taken back by their brazenness to continue the conversation right in front of me. Something sank inside me; I felt great sadness, like something had died. It felt like something had drastically changed. What my teammate had indirectly stated was that blacks were inferior to whites and that whites should not date blacks, especially not a white female athlete whom he found attractive. She, of course, should save herself for a white guy like him.

I immediately thought to myself, "How many other of my white teammates feel this way? Do they all feel this way? What about the team? What about family?" The message of "team" and "family" was now being challenged. The concept of my teammates being my brothers was challenged as well. And even though my teammate's comments about interracial dating were not directed at me, his comments and what he inferred about blacks, applied to me as well. From that point on, my coach's message about brotherhood and family seemed impotent. After that, whenever our coach referred to us as a "family" during a pregame speech or in a meeting, I tuned him out. What one of my teammates said and believed about blacks created disdain in my heart and mind; it challenged the validity of our coach's message.

The Message of the Gospel

The Bible tells us that God created a perfect world and created Adam and Eve to dwell in it. Adam and Eve disobeyed God and sinned by eating the fruit God had told them not to eat. Adam and Eve's disobedience brought sin and death into the world. From that point on, all of mankind was born into sin and deserving of eternal punishment from a Holy God.

Yet God loved mankind, so He sent His Son, Jesus to earth to die a death that would atone for the sins of the world and grant eternal life to those who believe in him. All those who receive him would be called Children of God and will spend all of eternity with God the Father. This is the message of the gospel.

Those who receive and believe the gospel are unified under its message. The apostle Paul in 1 Corinthians 12:27 refers to those who believe as the "Body of Christ." This group, though they are individuals, are one in Christ. Believers are unified by the work of Christ. The unity of this gospel message goes beyond ethnic and cultural distinctions. Paul says in verse 13, "For in one spirit we were all baptized into one body Jews or Greeks, slaves or free and all were made to drink of one spirit." Paul wants Christians to realize that nothing should separate them from their fellow Christians, regardless of their ethnicity. I believe this includes prejudice, racism, discrimination, and racial bias.

As a black Christian, when I hear or read racially pejorative remarks towards blacks from white Christians, it challenges the message of the gospel preached in predominantly white churches. It does not challenge the true purity of the message found in sacred scripture; rather, it challenges the purity of living out the implications of the gospel message. This is not a new chal-

lenge for black Christians: it is a challenge that has been present
for black Christians and black Americans for hundreds of years.
It was the dilemma that slaves confronted when they heard the
gospel from their white slave owners. The message was an incredible message, but the practical lived-out unity of the message
between white slave owners and their black slaves were two different things. How was a black slave to understand this message
in his/her daily interactions with white Christian masters? There
was something about the way white Christians lived out the message that left a stain on it.

The black Abolitionist, Frederick Douglass, said these words
in reference to Christianity:

> What I have said respecting and against religion, I mean
> strictly to apply to the slaveholding religion of this land,
> and with no possible reference to Christianity proper; for,
> between the Christianity of this land, and the Christianity
> of Christ, I recognize the widest possible difference—
> so wide, that to receive the one as good, pure, and holy,
> is of necessity to reject the other as bad, corrupt, and
> wicked. To be the friend of the one, is of necessity to
> be the enemy of the other. I love the pure, peaceable,
> and impartial Christianity of Christ: I therefore hate
> the corrupt, slaveholding, women-whipping, cradle-
> plundering, partial and hypocritical Christianity of this
> land. Indeed, I can see no reason, but the most deceitful
> one, for calling the religion of this land Christianity. I
> look upon it as the climax of all misnomers, the boldest
> of all frauds, and the grossest of all libels. Never was
> there a clearer case of "stealing the livery of the court of
> heaven to serve the devil in." I am filled with unutterable
> loathing when I contemplate the religious pomp and
> show, together with the horrible inconsistencies, which
> everywhere surround me.[1]

In Douglass's words we see the dilemma that black Christians
have faced for years and to some extent still face.

[1] Frederick, Douglass. *Life of an American Slave* (Boston: Anti-Slavery Office, 1845), p. 118.

An Example of this Problem

A few years ago, I received an email written by an honest white Christian brother. He disagreed with how I applied the word "inequality" in a talk I gave. In that talk, I mentioned that I believe many blacks still face inequality in America. His email explained his belief that blacks in America have the exact same opportunity as everyone else: there is no longer racial inequality.

I responded with an email mentioning poor public education and the American prison system. I explained that many of the failing public schools in America are made up of mostly, but not exclusively, black and Hispanic students. I then mentioned that in the American prison system there are about 2 million prisoners, and of that prison population, most are racial or ethnic minorities.[1] I said this seemed disproportionate because African Americans only make up about 13 percent of the U.S. population and Hispanics only make up about 16 percent of the U.S. population.

In response, he emailed stating he believed blacks and Hispanics were inherently more prone to criminal behavior than whites. This is what he believed accounted for the high incarceration rate among blacks and Hispanics. I was stunned by this response. I then wondered if my Christian brother thought I was more prone to criminal behavior than he was. At this point it became very difficult to feel like we were Christian brothers.

This interaction with my white Christian brother saddened me. Although his thoughts and views of blacks were not directed at me, I felt that they were, and this again made me wrestle with questions concerning unity in the body of Christ and the unifying message of the gospel. I asked myself questions such as: "How should the gospel of Jesus Christ inform my white Christian brother's attitude towards blacks and towards me as his black Christian brother? Are we really one member in Christ if these attitudes are in his heart? Did other white Christian friends feel this way about blacks? Is this the gospel message lived out among white and black believers?"

---

[1] Alexander, Michelle, *The New Jim Crow: Mass Incarceration in the Age of Colorblindness* (New York: The New Press, 2012), p. 6.

Paul and Peter

Racism and racial bias does violence towards the true message of the gospel. This is similar to a charge Paul levied against Peter, Barnabas, and a few other Jews, recorded in Galatians 2. Peter, a Jewish Christian, had been eating regularly with Gentile Christians, but when other Jewish Christians came to eat, Peter left the Gentiles to eat with the Jews instead. Paul observed Peter's actions and rebuked him publicly, calling him a hypocrite and critiquing his behavior. Paul wrote, "But when I saw that their conduct was not in step with the truth of the gospel . . ." (v. 14). What did Paul mean by saying that Peter and the others' actions were not in step with the truth of the gospel? The gospel message is that all Christians are justified by faith in Christ through his atonement for their sins—including Gentiles. Before Christ, the Jews observed food laws which forbid them from eating with Gentiles because they were considered ceremonially unclean. But when Christ atoned for sin, the separation between Jew and Gentile was removed, and they were made one in Christ. This is the gospel message. This is why Paul spoke against Peter's behavior. When Peter removed himself from eating with the Gentiles out of fear of what the Jewish Christians would think, he was acting as if the gospel message was not true. If the gospel message was true, he did not need to separate himself from Gentile Christians. In doing so, Peter's actions were contrary to the gospel.

The gospel says that we are united to Christ and to each other—regardless of race or ethnicity. This unity is not only an outward unity, but also a unity in our hearts. When we think or act in a manner that is contrary, we malign the gospel. So what is at stake? The gospel is at stake. Continued efforts towards racial reconciliation between white and black Christians can uphold and display the unifying message of the gospel.

The Need for Unity

Secondly, I believe there is much at stake because our country is quickly becoming a secular nation, a nation in which there is no longer a great social advantage in professing to be a Christian. Years ago, when I attended Covenant Seminary, professor Jerram Barrs warned that America was headed down the same path as France and Great Britain. What he meant was that both of those societies became incredibly secularized and the influence of Christianity, on a large scale, had waned, and in some places was non-existent. If America is headed down that path, and there are clear signs that we are, then the body of Christ in America will need to be more unified than ever before.

This means that white and black Christians will need to be united in a greater way to do the work of the Kingdom. The emotional racial divide will need to close or that divide will continue to be exploited, as it is often exploited during a political season. Politicians exploit Christians by pandering to their fears. If they can appeal to the fears of white and black Christians, then we will be deeply divided.

The political divide in our country seems to parallel the political divide between white and black non-Christians. One of the reasons this happens is because white and black Christians don't often discuss our true feelings about the political parties. For example, many black Christians support the Democratic Party because they feel that the Democratic Party has done and will do more for the advancement of blacks and underprivileged groups in America. Many white Christians support the Republican Party because they feel that the Republican Party will do more to advance social issues they support. As white and black Christians, we may never admit this, but there are many white and black Christians in America who feel this way. But when Christians in America no longer enjoy the benefits of being the dominant group in a society, we will need to be unified. We can disagree politically, but we can still be united.

If white and black Christians are not truly united, and the more secularized our culture becomes, the church will weaken, as will its influence in society. As the pressures of a secular society press in on the church, the fractures between white and black Christians will reveal themselves. Recent racial unrest in America should remind us that, as W.E.B DuBois said, "The problem of the 21st century is the problem of the color-line."[1] In other

---

[1] Du Bois, *The Souls of Black Folk*, V.

words, race is still a problem in America. And if America is still wrestling with issues of race, then the church will be confronted with those issues too. Yet, if white and black Christians commit to doing the hard work of racial reconciliation, the church will be a light to the nation in this area, and will be able to withstand the racial struggles of the nation.

Weary of Apathy

I am not only concerned the American church will divide in the future over the ongoing racial struggles in our nation, I am also concerned many black Christians might grow weary of the apathy they perceive in their white brothers and sisters towards racial injustice. Many black Christians who attend predominantly white churches often endure ignorance, disbelief, and resistance to the reality of systemic racism and racial bias. Often these black Christians feel isolated and lonely, not because their white brothers and sister are not friendly and loving, but because many of them are not aware or do not know how to encourage their black brothers and sisters.

For example, during the summer of the Trayvon Martin case, none of my white brothers or sisters from my church asked me or my wife what we thought about the case or how we felt about it. Perhaps they did not think about it or they did not know what to say—as is often the case. But this just highlights how isolated a black Christian can feel in a predominantly white setting. Black Christians understand that it does not even occur to their white brothers and sisters to ask how they are doing or to get their perspective on the situation. If they did, it would be encouraging. Yes, there are some black Christians who may not care whether whites inquire about them when the nation is embroiled in racial injustice, but I am sure they would appreciate the sentiment, especially if it is sincere. As a result, I wonder if many black Christians will head back to the black church or a multicultural church rather than stay in an environment that is hard to navigate.

There are many days my wife and I sit in church on Sunday and wonder if we should return to the black church. At the black church we would not feel isolated culturally and we would not have to wonder if the black members cared about issues of racial injustice. We would not have to try and convince the black members that America still has a race problem. We would not have to explain to our black members our fears about our black sons getting pulled over by the police. We would not have to wonder if they thought we were being dramatic about it. We would not have to wonder if the negative comments made about President Barak Obama are truly because of his policies or because his skin color is different from the other forty-three white American presidents. I do wonder whether returning to the black church might be better for my family and me; it would certainly be easier. Nevertheless, we have been called to serve where we are and we have made our peace with it. I do wonder though about other black Christians in America—will they remain part of predominantly white churches?

In a country where it seems the dialogue about race is increasing, the lack of conversations within predominantly white churches may communicate to black church members a message of apathy or avoidance. To this, many black Christians may respond by saying, "I cannot do this any longer" and leave to seek refuge in a black church and or a multicultural church that is committed to long-term racial reconciliation. I believe there are many black Christians who love their predominantly white church and do not desire to leave, even though they would agree that their church needs to address the issues of race in America. White churches will need to be courageous and intentional about providing opportunities for their members to grow in these discussions about race.

When white churches begin to engage in the difficult dialogue about race in America, it begins to establish some credibility among black Christians, particularly ones that attend that church. As black Christians, many of us never assume whites or white Christians will be motivated to really lean into difficult conversations about race—especially those conversations that may reveal unconscious bias by whites and white Christians towards blacks. Many black Christians never expect white Christians to preach about it, teach about it, talk about, ask about it, learn about it, or care about it. This was not something we were necessarily bitter or resentful about; rather, this was just what we experienced.

As a teen, I had many white Christian friends, which meant I was regularly in and out of predominantly white churches, even though I went to an all-black church. I went to the Methodist Church, the Southern Baptist church, the Christian church, the Presbyterian church, and the Assembly of God church. In all my teen and young adult years, I do not remember any conversations about race, institutional racism, or any sort of injustice towards African Americas. The topics never came up. The first time I ever heard the term 'racial reconciliation' in the context of a church was at a Promise Keepers rally in 1992. I remember reading one of the books that talked about vows the Promise Keepers were committed to keeping, and one of them was a commitment to racial reconciliation. I was so shocked that my mind had to wrestle with whether I thought racial reconciliation was something Christians should work toward. I almost saw it as something that someone should pursue outside of their Christian walk. I think the silence in many of these predominantly white churches I visited over the years sent the unconscious message that this was a secondary issue or even a tertiary one. However, I know the Christian life must be an integrated life and not a compartmentalized life. Again, I am not "throwing shade" or "condemning" my white brothers and sisters in those churches, because they loved me well. They just weren't thinking about issues of race or racial reconciliation. But this is a new day, and I am extremely hopeful for us. I am beginning to see white brothers and sisters being courageous enough to lean into the hard and difficult conversation of race in America.

There is a lot at stake. Most importantly is the unified message of the gospel. We don't want to malign or misrepresent the gospel to a watching world. Secondly, unity in the Christian church is at stake. If white and black Christians cannot find a way to commit to ongoing racial reconciliation and other social justice issues, there could be a greater division between white and black Christians in America. This would be most unfortunate because we are entering a time in our country's history when the church needs to be more unified than ever. We also do not want to see black Christians, who belong to predominantly white churches, leave in great numbers because they feel their church is not concerned about the issues that plague the black community. But I am hopeful. I am hopeful for better days for white and black Christians. I pray this book would facilitate conversation and help create a deeper unity between white and black Christians in America. May God bless us all.

Discussion Questions

1. What does the author say is at stake if white and black Christians do not do the hard and ongoing work of racial reconciliation? Do you agree or disagree?

2. The author mentioned many white Christians tend to vote Republican and many black Christians tend to vote Democratic. Is this true in your experience? If so, do you agree with the reasons mentioned?

3. Do you think racism is still a problem in America? Why or why not? Would any of your black friends or black Christian friends agree with you?

4. What are some reasons black Christians might grow weary in attending a predominantly white church?

5. Why does the author say he is hopeful?

Appendix A

A Letter to My Black Christian Brothers and Sisters

To my black Christian brothers and sisters:

Hey family, we must recognize the season we are in and steward it well. Our white brothers and sisters are ready to lean into the conversation of race and social justice issues that plague black communities. So we must be patient enough to talk with our white brothers and sisters and answer their questions. Most of my white brothers and sisters did not grow up having conversations about race, so these conversations can be very intimidating for them. As I said earlier in the book, many white Christians do not know what to say, they do not understand many of the issues that African Americans face, and they do not know what to do. The good news is, many want to learn. You will need to take time out to have coffee, lunch, or dinner with your white brothers and sisters and share your experiences and thoughts with them. Stories can be magical in bringing a greater level of understanding. You can also suggest books, resources, videos, conferences, and speakers that will help them grow. I am certain we need each other. So let us commit to being "quick to hear, slow to speak and slow to get angry" as we move forward in a way that we have never moved before.

Peace,

Aaron Layton

Appendix B

Racial Reconciliation Forum and Event Proposals (Examples)

Proposal 1

Event: West County Forum II
Title: Racial Reconciliation in the wake of Ferguson
Date: Saturday, May 27, 2017
Where: Friendly Temple Missionary Baptist Church
Time: 6:00-8:30 p.m.

Purpose: To gather black and white Christians together to heal and share over a family meal and to continue dialogue towards a greater racial understanding of one another.

Logistics:
1. We will invite the people and churches who attended the West County Forum on Ferguson "Why so much Anger?"
2. We will provide bus transportation for those from West County and transport them to FTMB and back.
3. We will begin the night with a welcome and prayer and then we will eat a family meal together. There will be basic "getting to know you" questions at the tables for the attendees to answer.
4. After dinner we will briefly lay a biblical and practical framework for reconciliation.
5. Then each table will be led by a table leader into a round table discussion about racism in America.
6. We will encourage white and black participants to exchange contact info with one another in order to develop ongoing relationships in which they can continue racial dialogue towards greater understanding and unity.
7. We will end with prayer at each table.
8. We will provide a resource and book list.

Proposal 2

Event: West County Forum III
Title: "Am I a defender of the poor and needy?"
"Open your mouth for the mute . . . defend the rights of the poor and needy." Prov. 31:8-9
Date: Saturday, August 19th, 2017
Where: Journey (West County)
Time: 6:30-8:30 p.m.

Purpose: To hear from white brothers and sisters who have been spiritually transformed through their service to vulnerable people who come from a different ethnic and socioeconomic background. The hope is that it would encourage a deeper engagement and commitment, from our congregation and other West County churches, to those who are vulnerable.

Logistics:
1. We will invite Andy Krumsieg (Jubilee), Jason Julian (Urban K-life), Shane Fast (Rebirth East St. Louis), Heather Marsee (Caring for an African American Male) and Pastor Barry Henning (New City Fellowship St. Louis)
2. Each speaker will be given 10 minutes to tell their story of spiritual transformation, and will conclude by answering the questions "Who are the mute?" "Who are the destitute?" "Who are the poor?" "How do we defend their rights?"
3. We will take a short break and then have our five speakers sit at five different tables and allow a group of people to sit and ask questions. After 12 minutes the people will rotate to another table with another speaker. Each speaker will pray over and lovingly challenge the group before they leave.
4. At the end of the time the speakers will head to the foyer were they will share specific opportunities for the people to get physically involved.
5. We will invite the people and churches that attended Forums I and II.
6. We will provide a resource and book list.

Proposal 3

Event: West County Forum IV (The Journey, FTMBC, New City Fellowship)
Title: "Selma"
Date: Friday, October 6th, 2017
Where: New City Fellowship Church
Time: 5:30-8:45 p.m.

Purpose: To continue racial reconciliation through dialogues about race with The Journey, a predominantly white church, and Friendly Temple, a predominantly black church, by way of the movie "Selma." (Eph. 2:11-22; 4:1-6; 1 Cor. 12:26)

Logistics:
1. We will invite our brothers and sisters from Friendly Temple Missionary Baptist Church to join us at New City Fellowship Church to watch the movie "Selma" and have a time of discussion afterwards. We will also invite New City Fellowship members and our members at other Journey churches.
2. We will encourage those from FTMBC and The Journey West County (WC), who connected at our forum in February to attend this meeting as a group. These groups will also sit together during the table discussion after the movie.
3. We will provide food (pizza, etc.) in order to encourage people that may be coming from work.
4. We will have table leaders to ensure everyone has an opportunity to talk during the table discussions.

Proposal 4

Event: Racial Reconciliation - West County Forum V
Title: "What do you mean by white privilege?"
"The Lord makes poor and makes rich . . ." 1 Sam 2:7
Date: Friday, November 25th, 2017
Where: Journey
Time: 6:30p-8:45 p.m.

Purpose: To define, reveal and discuss the meaning of the term "white privilege" and its implications for the Journey and evangelical churches America.

Logistics:
1. We will have the worship team from Grace Bible Church, an African American church in Florissant. We will open with two songs.
2. Pastor Scott will give a welcome and an introduction. Aaron Layton and Mike Leary will then each, individually, address the topic of "white privilege."
3. Aaron and Mike will lead the audience, or a few from the audience, in an activity designed to reveal privilege.
4. After a short break the audience will break into small groups for a discussion on white privilege.
5. Each group will have table leaders and a Journey pastor at each table.